2003

Career and Academic
Advising Center

# INTERNATIONAL BUSINESS

# EDWARD J. HALLORAN

SECOND EDITIC

D1534311

**VGM Career Books**

Chicago   New York   San Francisco   Lisbon   London   Madrid   Mexico City
Milan   New Delhi   San Juan   Seoul   Singapore   Sydney   Toronto

**Library of Congress Cataloging-in-Publication Data**

Halloran, Edward John.
　　Careers in international business / Edward J. Halloran.—2nd ed.
　　　　p.　　cm. — (VGM professional careers series)
　　Includes bibliographical references.
　　ISBN 0-07-140735-9
　　1. International business enterprises—Vocational guidance.　　I. Title.　　II. Series.

　　HD2755.5 H35　　2003
　　331'7'02—dc21

2002192422

1 2 3 4 5 6 7 8 9 0　　DOC/DOC　　2 1 0 9 8 7 6 5 4 3

ISBN 0-07-140735-9

Interior design by Robert S. Tinnon

McGraw-Hill books are available at special quantity discounts to use as premiums and sales promotions, or for use in corporate training programs. For more information, please write to the Director of Special Sales, Professional Publishing, McGraw-Hill, Two Penn Plaza, New York, NY 10121-2298. Or contact your local bookstore.

This book is printed on acid-free paper.

*In memory of Cathy and Jay Tarrant and Dick Murdy*

# CONTENTS

# FOREWORD

This foreword is written to congratulate all of you who have chosen international business as a vocation. You are entering an exciting field of enormous opportunity and challenge, particularly within the realm of free trade.

Free trade is something that I believe will, inevitably, change the way we do business throughout the world.

Consider the recent dramatic admittance of China to the World Trade Organization and Russia's rapidly expanding trade with the rest of the world. Both of these developments will open many previously nonexistent trade avenues to international companies.

While there are many free trade agreements being negotiated in the world today, I want to limit my comments to one of the most important free trade agreements ever proposed for those who live in the Western Hemisphere: the Free Trade Agreement of the Americas (FTAA).

An FTAA composed of all countries in the Western Hemisphere is a prospect that holds tremendous potential. It could create the strongest trading block in existence. Only Cuba, as a communist dictatorship, would be excluded.

The FTAA was the brainchild of President George H. W. Bush, in response to changed circumstances at the end of the Cold War. His administration negotiated the North American Free Trade Agreement (NAFTA), consisting of Canada, the United States, and Mexico. He promoted the Asia Pacific Cooperation Pact (APEC) and supported a free trade agreement with Chile. His push of the Uruguay global trade talks resulted in competitive efforts from the European Union (EU) to complete the global Uruguay Round trade negotiations. These historic events marked the beginning of unprecedented growth in free trade agreements.

But it is true that a rising tide raises all ships. No one can dispute the success of NAFTA when you look at the numbers. Trade among Canada, Mexico, and the United States, which in the 1990s was $230 billion, grew to $655 billion in 2000. In contrast, trade between the United States and the EU, which in 1990 was $190 billion, grew to only $384 billion in 2000. The trade gap between NAFTA and the EU is widening. In 2000, the United States had 71 percent more trade with its NAFTA partners than with the EU.

Under NAFTA, Mexico has increased exports from $61.4 billion in 1993 to $182 billion in 2000. Foreign direct investment in Mexico increased from $4.4 billion in 1993 to $13.5 billion in 2000. Contrary to concerns voiced by NAFTA's opponents in the United States, NAFTA has created jobs in all three countries. In the United States alone, it's estimated that 350,000 jobs were created due to NAFTA-related exports during the first five years of the pact.

Countries that engage in free trade and democratic reforms are much more prosperous. In Mexico, a middle class is slowly emerging, along with a more open and democratic society. The first opposition-party president in Mexico was elected in 2000, when Vicente Fox of the PAN party was elected president in a free election. Then-president Ernesto Zedillo, a member of the then-ruling party, the PRI, incurred the wrath of his party by guiding free and open elections, which cost his party's candidate the presidency.

Our current president, George W. Bush, has promised to bring the FTAA to fruition by 2005. He has a formidable task ahead of him. In 1994, when President Clinton began negotiations for an FTAA by hosting a Miami summit, North and South American leaders agreed to have the FTAA in place by 2005. However, fearful of alienating protectionist political constituencies, President Clinton was unwilling to build on NAFTA or even defend it. In 1997, the Democratic party in Congress refused to support him in his request for authority to negotiate any free trade agreements.

Lasting consequences remain as a result of this lack of support. Recognizing the strategic value of NAFTA, countries throughout Latin America were competing to negotiate free trade agreements with the United States in the 1990s. At that time, they wanted to connect their economies, societies, security, and even their political systems to the United States. But we failed to seize those opportunities, so Latin America has proceeded with its own customs union, negotiating new trade ventures with the EU and Japan.

Although Latin America remains dubious, the United States is moving forward. President Bush remains committed to the FTAA and has made it a priority of his administration.

An FTAA would unite the Western Hemisphere in ways we can barely imagine: visualize a tariff-free zone linking over 800 million people, producing over $11 trillion in goods and services, and creating the world's largest common market—far bigger than the European Union.

Imagine a hemisphere where all democratic countries have full access to each others' goods and services. Where closed economies are opened and citizens have the opportunity to work and achieve economic prosperity. Where mothers and fathers can support their families without crossing borders to find jobs. Where disputes between countries are settled by the rule of law and not by armies and border wars. Free trade just may hold this promise.

But that is fodder for a future book. In the meantime, it's up to the next generation (you!) to lead the world into the most open and free trade we have ever seen. Opportunities abound for those who are willing to make the commitment. I wish you good fortune and I trust your efforts will lead us down the path to global peace and prosperity.


GEORGE HEINRICH
PRESIDENT, HEINRICH ADVERTISING AND DIRECT MARKETING
CHAIRMAN OF THE BOARD OF DIRECTORS, CHAMBER OF THE AMERICAS

# ACKNOWLEDGMENTS

This book, now in its second edition, has taken on a life of its own through the years, and I'm grateful to a rather large number of people who have taken the time to make suggestions concerning its content.

The late John Tarrant was the first to recognize the need for this book, and Sarah Kennedy and Betsy Lancefield Lane worked long and hard to help me bring it into existence.

Robert Wing, the former president of IHS International, has been a constant source of useful information and suggestions, and the editors at VGM Career Books—particularly Denise Betts, Ellen Vinz, and Monica Stoll—have had a great deal to do with shaping the second edition.

Students, clients, and academic and corporate colleagues too numerous to mention here (although some of their names appear in the text) have also taught me a great deal, and I've attempted to include their ideas and address their concerns as I worked on this updated edition.

Finally, as ever, I'm indebted to my wife, Maria Cristina, for her love and support.

# INTRODUCTION

For simplicity's sake, citizens of the United States are described throughout this book as "Americans," but keep in mind that people from Central and South America view themselves as Americans, too.

More accurately, we are "North Americans" and are referred to this way by our fellow Americans to the south. (In Spanish, the feminine term is *norteamericana*, and the masculine version is *norteamericano*.) A useful way to remind ourselves of this is to remember that the United States is a member of the Organization of American States (OAS). While people from Europe, Asia, Africa, Australia, and even Canada (another OAS member) are likely to refer to U.S. citizens as "Americans," people from other countries in our region may find us offensive if we arrogate this term for ourselves.

## BE PREPARED

There are jobs in the international sector for U.S. and Canadian citizens, and all indications are that there will be many more as time goes by. Unfortunately, many Americans are often ill-prepared to compete for these positions. The fact is, many foreign nationals are better educated (except, perhaps, in the technical areas) than their American counterparts. First of all, foreigners tend to know their own language thoroughly, while functional illiteracy is fairly common in the United States. As a rule, Americans often do not write well, and this greatly reduces their employability in the international sector.

In addition to great facility in their own tongue, many foreigners in the business world also speak one or more foreign languages fluently. Meanwhile, the average American who has "studied" another language is hard pressed to get beyond observing, "My aunt's pen has fallen off the dresser."

English is the foreign language of choice for many people in the international business community, and they tend to speak it well. They are also fully conversant with geography and often know more about the world (including the United States) than do their American counterparts.

Americans can land international jobs, but to do so they must study harder on an ongoing basis. The world is in a constant state of political, economic, and social change, and people who want to succeed in what has become a global market for goods, ideas, and services will need to keep abreast of these changes.

This book is designed to help Americans prepare to compete for international positions. Many, but not all of these jobs, will be in sales and marketing. We will look at where the opportunities lie for a variety of positions, including traditional jobs, contract work, and increasingly, excellent opportunities for entrepreneurs.

Surprisingly, most of the opportunities for international work will be right here in the United States, and, in many cases, Americans will be working for foreign companies.

A well-prepared American has a great deal to offer a foreign firm, and challenging opportunities abound for people who are willing to continue to learn and grow. This book will provide a method for finding and keeping positions in the exciting world of international business.

## HOW TO USE THIS BOOK

The mere fact that you are reading this book indicates that you have given at least a little thought to looking into career opportunities in the international sector. This text will help you determine if you are truly cut out for a career in international business, and in the process you will be exposed to other possibilities you may not have thought of.

Salary ranges have been left out on purpose, because if a given career does not appeal to you on its own merits, you are not going to be happy for very long, no matter how much money you're making. When you are asked to answer questions, be honest with yourself. No one can help you unless you have determined what it is that you want to go after and what your strengths and shortcomings are.

The sources mentioned throughout the book will provide you with a great deal of useful information. However, understand that you are reading a primer and that you will need to do more research on your own.

Be open-minded as you read the book and in your subsequent pursuit of knowledge. Too often in the past, Americans have tended to take a narrow look at the rest of the world. It was tasteless then, and it is economic suicide now because we need other countries' business more than they need ours. In short, it behooves us to become better citizens of the world and open ourselves to new possibilities. And why not? It is not only good business, it is enjoyable!

C H A P T E R

1

# TODAY'S GLOBAL BUSINESS WORLD

**U**pon completion of this chapter, you should be able to:

- Appreciate the nature of change in the global economy
- Weigh the pros and cons of working in the international sector, given the expansion of terrorist activities
- Understand the nature of your competition for international positions
- Commit to a lifelong contract with yourself to continue to learn and grow

## FREE TRADE

While the expansion of NAFTA has, indeed, hurt some companies in the United States and Canada, it has also expanded many markets for U.S. and Canadian products, commodities, and, yes, workers. NAFTA, like the global economy itself, is all about change, and the inflexible will find themselves left behind. Happily, that doesn't need to be the case for you if you're willing to commit to a lifelong pursuit of knowledge (including learning new skill sets) and cultural growth, and that's what this book is designed to help you to do.

For several years I cochaired the marketing subcommittee of the Rocky Mountain chapter of the U.S.-Mexico Chamber of Commerce. I watched our leader, Gil Cisneros, build a vibrant group, and in the process, learn that in order to truly serve our region in the area of economic expansion, he'd need to expand his horizons. Together with George Heinrich, he founded the Chamber of the Americas, which is growing at a rapid rate.

During the 1997 Denver "Summit of the Eight" (the leaders of the G-7 nations and Russia), it became clear that many of the old barriers to trade were falling. A year later, NewTech '98, a Vatican-sponsored computer conference, brought together clergy and corporate executives from all over the globe with the goal of improving communications within the Roman Catholic Church, and with the secular world, knocking down additional barriers.

In today's wide-open global marketplace, even devalued currencies are no obstacle. For example, as a Russian businessman recently said to me, "The fluctuations of the ruble aren't a barrier to trade. We can provide certificates for timber, gold, and petroleum, all of which we have in abundance, and they're fully fungible."

China, according to Angel Chi, the president of the China Development Institute, is also firmly committed to Western-style marketing. "In 1999," Chi says, "China began their 'Western Development Campaign,' hoping to attract a combination of investors and experts in many fields. The program is ongoing, and is designed to boost the economy of China's western region—specifically the provinces of Shaanxi, Sichuan, Chongqing, Guizhou, Guangxi, Yunnan, Ningxia, Inner Mongolia, Gansu, Quinghai, Tibet, and Xinjiang. The need for expertise is ongoing, as China is going to host the Olympics in 2008, and realizes what a global showcase that will be. As a result, opportunities will expand during the years leading up to the Olympics."

This is a particularly exciting time to look for work in the international sector, as truly unprecedented opportunities are available.

## PROTECTIONISM

The term *global village* has been with us for some time now. The world's governments have begun to acknowledge that we are in a single, market-driven global economy. NAFTA and GATT are two relatively recent admissions that we are all inextricably intertwined with one another in a single marketplace, and that trade restrictions are ultimately self-defeating. So, ever so slowly, we are moving in the direction of truly free trade.

Protectionism withers in the face of economic reality. If what a company is doing is not cost-effective, even its domestic customers will ultimately shop elsewhere. The proliferation of Japanese cars in the U.S. market is a good case in point. For many years, the Japanese made cars for less money than their American counterparts—even during periods when Japanese autoworkers were being paid more than U.S. autoworkers—because Japanese factories were, to the greatest extent possible, using industrial robots.

In addition to effecting various economies in the workplace, the Japanese were more responsive to the needs of the American market, making changes in vehicle size and style as the market dictated. Meanwhile, American autoworkers criticized the Japanese and asked, "Why don't they buy our cars?" The "they" actually included not only the Japanese, but also people in the United States. On the domestic front, people were buying foreign cars because they were sick of Detroit's gas guzzlers. Meanwhile, people in Japan were not buying even the most prestigious U.S. cars—because in Japan, as in England, the steering wheel is on the right side of the car. U.S. automakers were trying to sell them typical American cars with the steering wheels on the left! We as a nation paid for this error, among others, with an unfavorable balance of trade.

Although the automotive industry's criticism of Japan was largely irrational, the Japanese have maintained restrictive barriers against foreign—chiefly U.S.—goods (including agricultural products) that are usually less expensive and often better than their Japanese rivals' offerings. This protectionism has hurt Japan, and slowly, accommodations are being made. But the process is painful because in Japan, as in other countries, powerful domestic groups such as unions and industry associations aggressively attempt to maintain trade barriers.

The barriers are, however, gradually disappearing, and major concessions have been made in recent years. You have only to look at the Japanese and other foreign-owned factories in the United States to understand that we are in a time of significant change, and that we need to prepare ourselves to deal with it.

Ray Morgan, an international marketer, made the following comments about protectionism: "Protecting the American automobile industry by permitting the engines to be made in the East, the bodywork in Mexico, and then installing Canadian-made seats in Detroit so the car qualifies as an 'American-made product' puts the cause of international marketing and 'free trade' back into the seventeenth century. . . . Manufacturers must produce a superior product with quality that will withstand competition from around the world. . . . We must think global markets, but first remove the invisible barriers."

## WHERE THE JOBS ARE

Just as American Express was pulled into the world of international banking many years ago when immigrants sent money orders that were meant to be used in the United States back to their families in Europe, more and more American firms have discovered that new markets are opening up to them overseas, which leads to more and more opportunities for Americans to work in the international sector.

However, the jobs are increasingly likely to be in the United States itself. This is because, in addition to adhering to foreign governments' dictates that the bulk of the employees of U.S. firms doing business there be locals, there are other valid reasons for not sending inexperienced Americans abroad. As a senior executive in a large firm's international department told me, "By letting local nationals serve as our primary contacts abroad, I eliminate the risk of having an American approach a prospective customer in the wrong way. I let the locals set things up, and I don't have to worry about them telling the wrong kind of joke or being too pushy. Overseas, as a general rule, people want to get to know representatives of commercial firms as people first, before business is ever discussed. Most Americans have a difficult time dealing with this and, in many cases, the cultural and linguistic knowledge required to open doors abroad requires many years of study—indeed, you might even say a lifetime."

I asked him, "Once opened, is there a place inside the door for an American?" He replied, "Yes, if he or she is an expert at something, such as technical knowledge or finance. Using the local nationals on an ongoing basis to smooth the way for them, Americans can make significant contributions."

## RISKS

A great deal has happened since the first edition of this book was published in 1996, and I'd be remiss if I didn't address the more negative aspects of what's transpired, specifically both domestic and international terrorism.

There has been an exponential increase in terrorist acts, not only overseas, but also in the United States. Assassinations, both political and gang-related, have long been part of the American scene, and the Oklahoma City bombing made it very clear that domestic terrorists are every bit as deadly as their foreign counterparts. Many places I've loved being in have been the venue for truly horrific acts—Tel Aviv, Haifa, Jerusalem, Paris, London, Cairo, Mexico City, Tijuana, Madrid, and Manila are just a few.

That said, if we're afraid to do things because of violent people, nothing worthwhile will ever be accomplished. Many people feel that living and working abroad are well worth the risks and that their lives are richer for those experiences.

Yes, terrorists will continue to ply their trade, both in North America and abroad, but, putting it mildly, if working in international business is your goal, don't be deterred—the rewards far outweigh the risks.

## ECONOMIC EXPANSION: WHAT THE EXPERTS SAY

Ray Morgan is a major international marketer in the specialty advertising industry. Here are some of the things he has to say about the global marketplace and the people who want to work in it:

*What's the nature of the United States' position in the global marketplace?*

Economic survival for the United States now means seeking new markets. We must sell what we do best—education, technology, and whatever manufacturing remains—to reach the purchasing power of the world. We can no longer 'just produce and ship it,' we must market ourselves in competition with the world. We can no longer influence by demanding change. For the first time in our economic history we must do the changing. We must learn the needs, wants, and desires of our global neighbors.

Angel Chi is the head of the Denver-based China Development Institute.

*China is considered a hot market for foreign workers. What should people who want to work there study?*

They should develop a good understanding of Chinese business etiquette and practices, which may differ from those of other cultures. They should also learn the history of their profession in China and get to know the background of the organizations they hope to be working with. Finally, be an expert in your field—a resourceful one!

*What careers are particularly promising for foreigners in China?*

Marketing, management, technicians, and project managers for manufacturers; investment managers; and educators.

*In which areas do the Chinese require local assistance in the United States and Canada?*

Product development, marketing (including sales), and management expertise within the local workplace.

## A COMMITMENT TO LEARNING

There is a growing demand for Americans to work in the international sector as entrepreneurs, contract workers, representatives, consultants, or that rapidly vanishing breed, "regular" employees. Success goes to people who are willing to make a lifelong commitment to the pursuit of knowledge. This pursuit begins by deciding to expand your horizons right now.

A good place to begin is with the concept of time. Our impatience hurts Americans again and again because, no matter where we do business around the world, the people with whom we come in contact have a different concept of time. They often value periods of silent reflection while we are in a hurry to get on with things; instead of considering silence to be productive, we assume that the other party's response to us is negative. To break the perceived logjam, we offer a concession, thereby weakening our position.

The late W. Edwards Deming, the Total Quality guru, found a receptive audience for his message in Japan. He was committed to pursuing perfection on a lifelong basis. This sat very well with people in every area of endeavor in Japan, but in America, Deming's homeland, the idealization of "quick fixes" held sway for many years. Meanwhile, in terms of achieving quality, Japanese manufacturers were far surpassing their American counterparts. After several decades, it finally occurred to U.S. firms that maybe there was something to total quality management after all.

Many firms imitated Deming, while others sought his counsel. Successful companies who committed themselves to the bulk of his principles and kept working on improving the quality of their goods and services benefited from the Deming method. Others, in the words of a manager who was interviewed by one of my students, "tried that Total Quality stuff for a while, but it just didn't work!"

If you are interested in a career in the international sector, be prepared to commit yourself wholeheartedly for the long term. This book does not offer any quick fixes because, in order to work effectively in international settings, you have to be a perpetual student—not only of other cultures, but your own as well.

This lifelong pursuit of knowledge is frequently fascinating and, on occasion, frustrating. There will be many challenging moments in your working life, but each one will present you with an opportunity to learn and grow. The knowledge that you are still evolving should encourage you greatly because it means that, while others have dropped out, you are still open to exciting new possibilities.

Your competitors will be found both here at home and abroad. In either case, they are individuals who have committed themselves to preparing for careers, rather than jobs, which means that they are looking at things from a long-term perspective. In order to compete with them you will need to make a similar commitment, as expressed in the contract at the end of the chapter.

## ASSESSING YOUR KNOWLEDGE

The following questions will help you evaluate your knowledge in areas important to a career in international business:

1. What foreign country or countries would you like to work in?
2. How well do you speak the language(s)?
3. How sound is your knowledge of the country's physical, human, and economic geography?
4. How extensive is your knowledge of the country's customs, traditions, and history?
5. How does conducting business there differ from the way it is done in the United States?

First, make an honest assessment of your answers to these questions. At this point, how desirable are you as a potential representative of a U.S. firm in the country or countries you have listed? Then, go back and answer questions 2 through 5, assessing your knowledge of the United States. This will give you an indication of what you have to offer a foreign firm as a U.S.-based representative.

### Action Plan

Even without going away to school, there are things you can do right now. Start by conducting the following exercises:

1. List the places where you can study the language or languages you need. Note time commitments and costs.

2. Write a two- or three-page report on how business is transacted in a country that appeals to you. Compare and contrast the country's customs with those of the United States.

3. Write another two- or three-page report outlining the economic future of the country you wrote about in the previous report. What is the country's economic outlook? Who is likely to do well there?

4. Make a list of at least five U.S. firms that are doing business in the country you have been writing about. Check out their websites. If these

firms are publicly held corporations, contact them and request their annual reports and 10Ks.

5. Having read the reports you obtain, pick the most desirable company and draft a letter to the head of its international department. In it, say why you feel the company is a good place for you to work. Indicate what you have studied, both formally and informally, and outline your plans for future studies. Lay the draft of the letter aside for a few days. Then, read it and ask yourself if you would give the writer of that letter a follow-up call had such a letter arrived at your office. If the answer is yes, proof the letter carefully and send it to the company with your resume. If your answer is no, ask yourself why you are not a person they would like to talk to at this point, and how you can become such a person.

## Your First Contract

Please read the following contract. It is the starting point for your quest for a true career in the international sector. As with any other first step, many surprises will follow, If you are serious about a career in international business, you will greet the surprises as exciting challenges and do your best to meet them. If you can commit to this learning process, it is likely that you will succeed in international business.

I promise myself that I will keep an open mind as I survey the international sector for career possibilities. This will include acknowledging the fact that I may be deficient in one or more aspects and then doing something positive to bring myself up to an acceptable level. I realize that I will be dealing with different customs, traditions, and languages, and I promise that I will learn to appreciate these differences as valid alternatives to my own culture. Finally, I pledge that I will continue to strive to learn more about my own culture as well as the ones I will be dealing with throughout the course of my career.

_____
Signature and Date

2

# LANGUAGE, CULTURE, AND COMMUNICATIONS

**A**fter reading this chapter, you should:

- Have a better appreciation of the need to learn more about other cultures
- Have the opportunity to implement a plan of action to start your learning process
- Be able to discuss basic considerations in the areas of cross-cultural communications

## CONDUCTING BUSINESS IN DIFFERENT CULTURES

Each nation presents a different selling proposition. In order to sell yourself first, and eventually your company's products, you need to learn how business is conducted in that country.

Our way of doing business in the United States works very well for us. We tend to get on a first-name basis very quickly, and then we immediately begin to talk business. We are bottom line–oriented and, because "time is money," we do not "waste" it with a lot of "meaningless chatter."

We also do not feel comfortable with long periods of silence. That isn't a problem in the United States, because the person across the desk from us does not like silence either and is ready to begin talking the moment we stop.

We're always busy thinking, deciding what we will say next, just as soon as the other person stops talking. Instead of listening to what a person is saying, we concentrate on our next snappy line and listen for the split second of silence that will provide us with the opportunity to say it aloud.

People in other countries feel uncomfortable with our haste to transact. They also tend to be more formal than we are, and they value their privacy. So, as a general rule, they prefer a gradual, "getting to know you" process before getting down to business, at least when we're in their country.

Silence to many foreigners is a sign that they're engaging in reflective thought prior to speaking again, and the failure to acknowledge and practice these customs will hurt our chances of negotiating successfully when we're overseas.

## Language Is the Key to a Culture

The more time we devote to learning a language, the more we will appreciate the heritage, customs, and traditions of the country where we wish to do business. Remember that our own language is constantly evolving and our growth as English speakers should be lifelong. That being the case, we need to be patient with ourselves when it comes to studying another language. Full mastery, even in the course of a lifetime, is unlikely, but we should always be improving.

The mark of a truly educated person is not how much they know, but their awareness of how much they have yet to learn. A good education cannot teach you "everything." What it will do is provide you with the tools to pursue knowledge on a lifelong basis. Interesting people are those who continue to learn and grow. In the international sector, the more vigorously you are pursuing knowledge, the more intriguing people will find you and the more respect they will have for you. Once that happens, meaningful business relationships inevitably ensue.

## Cross-Cultural Communication

It may be helpful to see what a longtime international professional has to say about communicating with organizations and individuals in other lands. The following material on cross-cultural communication was contributed by David Johnson, who spent many years living and working overseas, initially as a translator and subsequently as a broadcast journalist. Today, he runs an advertising and public relations firm in Minnesota.

In business, many people interact daily with people in other countries. This interaction can take different forms, from E-mails and letters to telephone calls and personal meetings. The understanding of how to communicate with people in different cultures influences effectiveness. It is imperative to make sure that your first words in any form of communication succeed. Hopefully, all of your subsequent communications will help you to work successfully with others in the global marketplace.

After the breakup of the Soviet Union, a friend of mine, Vadim Branitski, served as a consultant to a group of American entrepreneurs traveling to the Republic of Georgia. Vadim is fluent in Ukrainian, Russian, and English. One member of his group also spoke these languages, but the rest were only proficient in English. At one point, an issue split the two groups, and the Georgians went to a corner of the room and began discussing the issue in their language. Not understanding what was being said, but sensing an opportunity, Vadim began speaking in Ukrainian with the other Ukrainian speaker in his group.

Hearing them, the Georgians stopped their conversation and asked what Vadim and his associate were discussing. Vadim replied, "The same thing you are talking about." At this point, the Georgians, unsure whether they had been compromised, returned to the negotiations. Vadim's approach succeeded in answering the three key questions dealing with cross-cultural communications:

- With whom are you communicating?
- What do you know about them?
- What is your message?

In Vadim's case, he knew that he was communicating with Georgians. He also knew that they were using their language to limit communication. His message, which he got across by speaking in

Ukrainian, was that it was critical for everyone to recognize the importance of talking together.

## Action Plan

To enable you to be effective and consistent in your communications, implement the following strategies.

First, always know who you are communicating with. This is particularly important when considered in a cultural context. Today in the United States, business communication often wanders between formal and casual limits. With many cultures, this would be neither professional nor acceptable. Many people are proud of their professional attainments and, within their own cultures, are respected for their position. A casual approach to communicating with them will likely achieve negative results.

You need to know the individual's actual title, his or her role in the organization, and have a good idea of how this person will help you attain your goal. If you've only heard a name, you must check to be sure that you have the correct spelling prior to sending written communication. Further, just knowing these basics about the individual will give you important clues about how to correctly address him or her and the tone of the language you'll use in framing your message.

Next, learn as much as possible before you communicate. This is a multilayered issue. You want to know as much as you can about the individual, the organization itself, and the country where the firm is located. These are all interrelated and the information is not difficult to obtain, thanks to the Internet and other sources.

Information about geography, language, history, and current developments is readily available in libraries and on the Web. If you wish to focus on a specific country or language, consider taking or auditing courses at a local college or university.

The Internet is also an excellent source of information about businesses because many of them maintain websites. In addition, you can frequently obtain information by writing to their marketing, sales, or public relations department.

Your information about the person you're communicating with may initially be limited to name, gender, title, and role. However, that's still enough to make sure that your first words will succeed. If your interaction is in person, you will immediately acquire information about the person's age. In many cultures, this information is especially significant in terms of how that person is regarded by others and should be regarded by you.

Clearly express your intended message. You should know what you want to say, and the message should provide a benefit or necessary information to the company with which you wish to associate.

If you grew up in the United States, you may be surprised to learn that people in many countries probably spent more time learning English than you did. They know how to use the English language properly and they expect those whom they deal with in a professional capacity to be especially knowledgeable.

The fact that you are a native speaker of "American" English means that you can easily express yourself in our culture. It does not mean, however, that you will be easily understood by someone from another culture. Take the time to think things through before communicating and use plain language; avoid slang and unexplained acronyms.

If you're engaging in written communication, check your text by using a dictionary from the United Kingdom rather than the United States. Learn the time zone of the company you're dealing with and send your communications to arrive at an appropriate time. If you live in either the United States or Canada, take advantage of the opportunities your multicultural nation provides to learn about other people. Resident subcultures are an excellent source of information about language, customs, traditions, geography, and approaches to business. Finally, if you actually go to work in another country, become aware of the fact that attitudes towards work differ among cultures. In many countries, it is important to develop a good personal rapport before commencing work. Also, expectations regarding overtime will often differ.

I recall hearing from a friend in Italy that the difference between Italians and Americans is that "Americans live to work, while Italians work to live." His statement is not a value judgment on the quality of work performed by either Italians or Americans, but a statement about their different attitudes toward work itself. As another example: Canada and the United States share both a border and at least one language, but there are likely to be more formal expectations in Canada regarding dress and dining among business professionals. These and other culture-specific factors can influence how effective you are in communicating with others.

### Fluency

Reasonable fluency and continued study of the host country's language or languages is virtually mandatory. This does not mean that fluent Americans will ultimately reach a point at which they can negotiate deals unaided—the individuals who can do this are rare because of legal, linguistic, and cultural complexities—but continued improvement in the host country's tongue shows a respect for the country's culture and is greatly appreciated.

An American woman who brokers deals in Eastern Europe told me, "Down through the years, through frequent travel and formal study, I've turned my high school German and a smattering of Polish into a fair degree of fluency. I still make laughable grammatical errors, but the people I'm transacting with are trying out their English on me, and sometimes it's pretty funny, so we laugh together and keep on trying. I'll always need interpreters for hammering out the details of contracts, but my continued improvement in spoken languages has solidified my business relationships."

The people who succeed in the international sector "know what they don't know," and do something about it.

## DON'T LIMIT YOURSELF

While fluency in a language is a definite plus in today's business marketplace, what is critical is that we be flexible and realize that we should not limit ourselves solely to that language and the country or countries where it is spoken.

An international marketing executive told me that a lot of Americans tend to sell themselves short in this regard. He cited a resume and cover letter he had recently received: "The writer had two years of German in high school and two more in college. The cover letter went on and on about the writer's appreciation of Germany and its heritage, although nowhere in the letter or resume was there any indication that he had ever even visited the country!" He added, "The letter talked about how he'd like to represent us in Germany, and left the door closed to any other possibilities. I tossed it." And why not? Let's look at where the writer went wrong:

- Focusing on Germany only. As the executive said, "What if we're not hiring anyone to work in Germany?"
- Claiming expertise concerning a given country, without having actually been there! I tend to feel that, even if he'd spent a week there as part of a student group, he would have referred to it as "having traveled extensively throughout the country."
- Failing to see that having mastered the rudiments of one foreign language would make the study of other languages somewhat easier.

A better approach would have included researching the company more thoroughly before contacting the executive. If the writer had done his homework, he would have learned that the firm's management hired local nationals to represent them overseas, but that they were looking for entry-level people in their international department—people who had studied a foreign language and who were willing to take advanced studies in it, or even learn another language, all at the company's expense. International travel would have eventually ensued, but not until the individual had been properly trained.

He would have been better advised to have written something along these lines:

"I have completed four years of German, two at the college level. I am fluent and constantly striving to improve. While I would prefer working in this language, studying it has proven to me that I have a facility for languages and that I enjoy learning about other cultures. So I am open to other possibilities if there is no vacancy in your German operation."

This kind of approach would have earned him an interview, which is the purpose of sending a cover letter and resume, and he would have been in the running for a position. Instead, he didn't make it past the initial screening.

### Action Plan

What follows is a series of steps designed to help you learn about another culture. This example deals with the French, although the model can easily be applied to any other culture. It begins with language, because if there's more than one way of saying something, there's obviously more than one way of thinking about it. Appreciating the inherent validity of another person's take on things is a definite plus in the international sector.

### *Week One*

Check out a set of language tapes from your local library—Passport Books's *Just Listen and Learn Business French* is one of the many good ones. Memorize basic greetings and the words for your favorite foods and beverages. Also, while you are at the library, check out a copy of Theodore Zeldin's *The French* (which is in English) and read any two chapters that interest you.

### *Week Two*

Continue to work with the language tapes, concentrating on the sections dealing with food and drink. Read a French publication (online, if necessary). *Paris Match* is a good choice. Make a list of the words that have the same spelling in English as they do in French. Try to get the gist of the articles and advertisements.

### *Week Three*

Visit a French restaurant and try out your vocabulary as you order.

### *Weeks Four and Beyond*

Enroll in a basic French course. If there is a waiting period, fill in the time by listing French words that have made their way intact into our language, including the names of cities, rivers, lakes, and so on. (This will keep you from experiencing ennui!) Revisit the French restaurant and try preparing

French dishes at home. Check out recordings in French (Edith Piaf, Charles Aznavour, "Tales of Hoffman," et cetera), and videotapes of films and travelogues. Whenever a French film is being shown locally, go. And, if there is a branch of the Alliance Française nearby, join.

What you have done is put yourself in motion, to begin to learn about the French language and culture. Music, literature, film, food: these are all critical elements of a culture, and they are fun to experiment with.

By taking this course of action, you are opening yourself to new experiences and possibilities, and you are making yourself more employable in the global job market.

## Other Courses of Action

Look for a "temp" position abroad. Manpower and Randstad are two major firms that come readily to mind. Check out their websites to see if they have offices in countries that appeal to you. Write to specific branches to see what they're looking for in terms of temporary workers, and find out what legal hoops you'll have to jump through in order to work overseas.

Online courses are an option if your schedule and/or location precludes your attending conventional classes. According to Dr. Kurt Miller, M.D., "I've had the pleasure of teaching people in Bosnia, Iceland, Korea, Australia, Japan, Hawaii, and many of the contiguous forty-eight states. Most of these students did not have access to quality education in an asynchronous environment prior to the advent of online education. . . . Are online courses the wave of the future? No, they are here now, and administrators and faculty must continue to develop programs that cater to the online learner or risk becoming irrelevant to a significant portion of the population." To sum it up, many schools are now offering online classes, so there's no excuse for not taking the courses you need.

I advise taking online courses from accredited schools, colleges, and universities. The range of courses available is broad and continues to expand. If your schedule permits, you may feel more comfortable taking certain types of courses, such as language classes, in person. In some cases, though, there's no other way but online to take a class, due to time constraints, travel, or other reasons. In those situations, being able to continue your education online is a tremendous advantage.

Guidance counselors, education officers, and friends and associates who have taken or are taking online courses are all potential sources of information when it comes to learning about what's available.

## PREPARING TO WORK OVERSEAS: WHAT THE EXPERTS SAY

Jaime Ong, Ph.D., was for many years a senior marketing executive for an Asian food and beverage conglomerate. Here are some of the things he has to say about preparing to work overseas.

*What's the best way for Americans to prepare for working overseas?*

Preparation comes to naught unless one begins with three attributes: first, a refusal to assume that whatever worked in one's previous company or country will work just as well in the next; second, a willingness to listen and learn; and third, a sense of humor. This observation applies not just to Americans, but to anyone working in a new environment. Some of our horror stories have to do with managers joining us after impressive careers in American companies and assuming that, given their credentials, they could make brilliant unilateral decisions that would leave the natives gasping in awe.

*Are there social considerations in terms of preparing to work overseas?*

On the matter of social preparation, one would do well to first, learn about the host country; and second, learn about the company. The employee's spouse should take part in this preparatory activity, as she or he is bound to experience a greater feeling of loneliness and vulnerability than the employee, whose work environment creates a natural network and source of social support. It goes without saying that a crash course of fifteen lessons of spoken Mandarin is hopelessly inadequate as preparation for an assignment in Shanghai; the ideal preparation would entail staying in the country and learning about the customs, history, business laws, and so forth before being given a full-time job in it.

Ray Morgan is a major international marketer in the specialty advertising industry.

*Could you sum up the requirements of global marketing?*

Global marketing requires international planning, culture and language education, and the access codes to these new markets. We must be integrated into the social and economic structure of places such as Moscow, Bangkok, and Sidi Slimane. The demand for talent to serve these markets opens the greatest opportunity for this land since the days when our predecessors carved a nation out of the wilderness. We're in a global economy, and we must prepare ourselves to serve it.

# 3

# CAREER GOALS AND ATTAINMENT

**U**pon completion of this chapter, you should be able to:

- Identify the educational and experiential requirements you will need for positions in the international sector
- Determine which type of training is likely to be the most productive for you
- Assess your life experience with an eye toward making yourself more marketable in the international sector
- Prepare a portfolio that will enable you to begin seeking work in your chosen field

## WHAT DO YOU WANT TO DO?

A student said to me recently, "I've been reading the classifieds in the papers, and I can't find any jobs that appeal to me. Is there a better place to look?" I told her that there are lots of places to look, including the Web, but it helped to know first what she was looking for. She replied, "A better job."

I asked what she meant by "better." It turned out that she really had not thought things through. In fact, that had been a pattern throughout her working life. She had drifted from job to job, leaving each to take a "better" position that turned out to be either the same as the one she had left, or even a little worse.

Personnel professional Gwen Lawton says this is common: "When I look at many applications under the heading 'Reason For Leaving,' it will say, 'To take a better job.' When I assess what they left and what they went to, it quickly becomes apparent that they were making a lateral move at best and often taking a step or so down."

People frequently become restless on the job. For any number of reasons, the job is no longer satisfying and we want to do something else, sometimes almost anything else. This is not surprising, because many jobs—even glamorous ones—are quite repetitive.

Years ago, I attended a briefing on awarding college credits for working experience. The gentleman conducting the session said, "Someone tells us he has seventeen years' experience in the electronics industry, and he wants credit for it. Our question to him is, is it seventeen years of different experiences, or seventeen times one?" The point is well taken. Down through the years, I have had students who fumed that their years of experience did not yield the academic credits they had expected. They seemed to expect to be rewarded for showing up on the job each day for all those years, even though their position really could be described as "times one."

Many positions are routine. (The beauty of working in the international sector is that you never run out of new things to learn about the cultures you are dealing with.) The fact is, that while my student had been working at a variety of jobs for a number of years, she had yet to enter a career field and had simply been drifting.

I drafted a questionnaire for her and told her that she was the only person who knew the answers. The questionnaire is reproduced here for your use. You will find it a convenient way to determine your interests and your initial qualifications for a career in international business.

## Career Goal Questionnaire

1. Where do you want to be ten years from now?

   Position

   _____

   Geographic location

   _____

Salary range

_____

2. Where are you now in relation to those long-term goals?
   Position (factor in education and experience)

_____

   Geographic location

_____

   Salary range

_____

3. Can you attain the aforementioned goals by remaining with your present employer?

_____

4. Can you attain some of those goals if you stay with your employer for a while longer?

_____

   If yes, which goals?

_____

   How long will you have to remain with your employer in order to reach these preliminary goals?

_____

5. If there is no chance for reaching any of the goals by staying where you are, should you remain while you gather educational credits?

_____

   If the answer is yes, what do you need to do in order to bolster your educational credentials?

_____

_____

If the answer is no, what is your plan for getting into a position that is more conducive to attaining your goals?

_____

_____

_____

The following detailed questions will help you to further explore your career options.

When you project yourself forward ten years and visualize your ideal career, do you honestly know:

- What people in that field do all day long?
- What education and experience you need to qualify?
- What the future projections for that field are?

Think about precisely where you want to be living ten years from now. Then answer these questions:

- What firms that are likely employers are located there?
- How likely are the above firms to remain (and expand)?
- With whom will you be competing for employment?
- How comfortable would your significant other/family be living there?
- Determine what salary you need. Then consider the following:
  - What does your dream position actually pay?
  - What do you have to do in return? For example, research relocation practices—how many moves are expected, and how frequently do you have to move?
- Are you willing to travel? If so, find out:
  - Where
  - How often
  - For how long
- After careful consideration answer the most important questions: Is it worth it to you? To your spouse and family?

## Special Considerations

You also need to consider how many hours you will be putting in, even while you are at home. Do those hours allow you sufficient time for your personal life? If not, you may want to rethink your goals.

My student found the questions on significant others particularly relevant. She said, "A few years ago when I was single, I would have been willing to relocate just about anywhere. But now, I'm married with two kids. My husband likes his job, and we like our house. While I really want to work in international business, I don't want to move!" Happily, her state, Colorado, has many opportunities for her to work with an international firm or to serve as a contract rep for a foreign firm, so she can be based in her own home city. However, travel would be a must. That did not pose a problem for her—provided, she said, "I'm not away all the time."

Travel requirements vary from one position and organization to another. I once had a corporate marketing job that had me flying all over the United States and Canada. I was on the road three weeks out of every four. It was a tremendous experience, but I gave up a great deal in return for it. Putting it mildly, I didn't have a life outside of the corporate world. For a time, that did not matter, but it does matter to me now, and I have no interest in doing such extensive traveling again for any amount of money.

## EDUCATION

What are the educational requirements for the career you have chosen? Educational options include junior colleges and technical training schools, four-year undergraduate colleges and universities, and graduate schools. In each case, it is important to choose your school carefully.

## Choosing a School

As a prospective student you are valuable to schools, so be certain that you shop around before enrolling in a program. School guidance counselors and reference librarians can help steer you in the right direction in choosing a school, and the schools you are thinking of applying to should be able to give you information concerning financial aid. The list of reference books in this chapter's "Action Plan" will also prove helpful.

In addition to your library research, check out the school through its graduates and their employers. Schools should not have anything to hide when it comes to this, so feel free to ask them for a list of graduates, including recent ones, and contacts in the personnel departments of prospective employers that have hired graduates of the school. Don't be shy about this! Your career is at stake, after all, and you are also about to commit to perhaps a year or more of training at the school.

Ask the school's graduates the following questions:

- How important was your training at your school in terms of landing you a job?
- How relevant is that training in terms of what you are actually doing now?
- How well prepared are you for the future as a result of your training?
- If you had it to do over again, would you go to the same school or another one? Why?

Ask personnel representatives from firms employing the school's graduates these questions:

- How have graduates from this school performed on the job?
- How relevant was the training they brought to their first jobs with you?
- Are there other schools of the same type that you respect more?
- Do you foresee an ongoing need for more graduates for positions with your company?

Be aware that many schools will pressure you to enroll, and that they may make all sorts of promises. Take your time in making your choice and be sure you're comfortable with your decision.

The following horror story illustrates the need to take care when choosing a school. A few years ago, I was offered a job as a part-time marketing instructor. I was all set to accept, but then I was told, "And you'll also be teaching accounting." When I pointed out that, while I had some training in the area, I did not consider myself to be qualified to teach accounting, I was told that the position required teaching both subjects and, after all, "The answers to all the problems are in the instructor's manual, so you'll be all set." I responded, "That's all well and good, but I'm not certain that the answers to the students' questions are in my head!"

I refused the job. I did ask, though, what they planned to do. The director said, "We have resumes on file from several accounting teachers and I'm sure that one of them will be willing to teach marketing too, so there's no problem." I pointed out that marketing and accounting are frequently in strong opposition to each other in the corporate world, and that two teachers were really necessary in order to present both perspectives. The director replied, "Oh, that doesn't really matter all that much!" That is precisely the type of school you need to avoid. Happily, that "business college" has since closed its doors.

### Junior Colleges and Technical Schools

Do you need additional technical knowledge? If so, a junior college or technical school may be right for you. Both degree and certificate programs are available.

A word about two-year degrees for undergraduates: generally speaking, people from other countries value education a great deal. Frequently, I'm asked by undergraduate students if they should complete the requirements for an associate's degree or just concentrate on their four-year degree. My advice is, if you can get a two-year degree on your way to a B.A. or B.S., do it. In many cases, students' tuition is being paid by their employers. When times get tough, education budgets are frequently slashed, so it pays to get a degree after your name as quickly as possible.

Although the completed credit hours may be exactly the same, there is a considerable perceptual difference between having "two years of college" and holding a two-year degree. The former description sounds like the student has not made up his or her mind yet about a career, while the latter indicates that the person finishes what he or she starts and has successfully completed the requirements for an accredited degree.

### Four-Year Undergraduate Programs

A bachelor's degree is frequently a minimum requirement for people who are seeking to enter business fields. This is particularly true in the international sector. Earning a degree indicates a serious commitment and the ability to complete a rigorous program. Obeying the dictum "Be an expert," your undergraduate pursuits may be devoted to something quite specific, such as accounting or computer information systems. If that is the case, be sure to include at least one foreign language among your electives.

History, geography, sociology, religion, literature, and so on may also be taken as electives. These courses are all designed to improve students' awareness of and appreciation for various cultures, including their own.

### Graduate Programs

Graduate school is very different from undergraduate studies, and I urge you to start by taking at least one course. Taking it a course at a time will let you get acclimated, and even if your employer won't pay for an advanced degree, the company might be willing to pick up the tab for one or more courses that will help you do better in your present position or prepare you for the next rung on the ladder.

A warning is in order here: Many students who have just completed their four-year degree want to take a break. Unfortunately for many, the months quickly turn into years, and they still have not started graduate school. This is particularly inexcusable if your employer will pay for some, if not all, of a graduate degree program.

### Action Plan

You should address your educational needs by first gathering information on various schools. Your reference librarian should be able to get you started, and most (if not all) of the books on the following list should be available at your library:

- Peterson/Thomson's *2 Year Colleges*
- Peterson/Thomson Learning's *The College Board College Handbook*
- Thomson-Peterson's *Competitive Colleges: Top Colleges for Top Students*

These guides, along with suggestions from guidance counselors and others, will get you started on checking out the schools. Follow up by looking at their websites, and when you find an interesting school, order their catalog. For information on careers, ask for VGM Career Books' *Occupational Outlook Handbook* and their *Big Book of Jobs*.

In addition, if you have decided that you will need to move to another city to make yourself more employable, ask the reference librarian to direct you to a publications guide that will give you the names, addresses, and phone numbers of daily papers (note: there may be just one) in your target city. Call, E-mail, or write to the circulation department of one or more to arrange for a subscription to their Sunday edition.

Your subscription to the Sunday paper, and checking out the daily editions on the Web, will teach you things that you will not find in a brochure from the Chamber of Commerce. Let's look at the Sunday paper, section by section:

- **International and national news.** How thoroughly do they cover these areas? Are there locally generated stories on a regular basis? If so, it is a good sign in terms of local sophistication.
- **Business.** Once again, look for national and international stories and features (including syndicated ones) in addition to the usual local, state, and regional fare. How much awareness of international issues is displayed in this section?
- **Editorials.** Do the regular and guest editorials reflect an appreciation for the importance of international business in general and in increasing local participation in the international marketplace?
- **Real estate and rentals.** What is the housing market like compared to where you're living now? What do apartments rent for?
- **Help wanted.** Who's hiring? Do they provide salary ranges in their ads?
- **Retail advertising.** What do the items (including food) you normally purchase cost in this city?
- **Community calendar.** What sort of activities take place that you would enjoy? How often?
- **Letters to the editor.** Do the writers address news topics as well as sports?

All of the above will provide you with an overview of what life is really like in your target city. That way, you will not be going in blind to its shortcomings, and you will also have a much better feel for the good elements of life in that locale. The information a newspaper can provide is very valuable. Make the small investment it requires.

## IDENTIFY AND STRENGTHEN YOUR SKILLS

"Be an expert" is sound advice. But how do you become an expert when no one is hiring? Well, you can start at zero and really develop your qualifications over a period of time. The fact is, though, that most of us do not start at zero. We tend to have some marketable skills, but we probably do not value them as much as we should. This is particularly true of skills that come easily to us.

It is time for you to create a career inventory for yourself. Include everything, from your freshman year in high school forward, that might help you land a job.

### Academic and Other Learning

Every course with career implications you have taken should be included in your inventory. This also includes nonscholastic training, such as seminars at work and training sessions conducted by various groups and individuals. These courses should be grouped by category, rather than dates, although you should note the dates you completed the courses. At first glance, a given course may not be construed as job-related. Let's look at the critical categories:

Technical training
Communications (written and oral)
Foreign languages
History
Sociology
Anthropology
Geography
Economics
Geopolitics
Business

If you have old textbooks and handouts, keep them. Also save relevant books and materials from courses you are taking now and in the future.

Newspaper and magazine articles, including those on the Web, can be of significant value in keeping your knowledge current. Check the television listings for relevant programs and watch or tape them.

It is also worth your while to listen to National Public Radio's "Morning Edition" and "All Things Considered." These programs will give you the kind of in-depth news that people in other countries take for granted. If you have access to a shortwave radio (try the Web, too), listen to English-language newscasts from other countries, and you will appreciate just how little news we actually get in the United States.

Your initial training in the areas listed earlier provided you with a methodology for pursuing knowledge on a lifelong basis. It is up to you to do this. Keep in mind that people from other countries appreciate the process of acquiring knowledge and respect individuals who are committed to learning. They know education does not stop when you earn a certificate or a degree. In fact, that's why graduations are referred to as "commencement exercises," because the graduates are making a new beginning.

Reviewing what you have already studied is both an encouraging and a humbling exercise. Like the rest of us, you are humbled by acknowledging how much you don't know. At the same time, you are greatly encouraged by that realization because your education has provided you with the means for going after that knowledge. You will never learn everything, but the ongoing pursuit of knowledge is its own reward, as you will derive enormous satisfaction every time you realize you have learned something new and significant.

In an ideal world, every time we come across a box where we are to write in our occupation, we would use the word "student," because we should all strive to learn more and more. Unfortunately, many people conclude that their education stopped when they left school.

People who have stopped learning hold no interest for foreign professionals. People from other countries are amazed when they meet Americans who are not availing themselves of the readily accessible training the United States offers. Frankly, if you are not continuing to learn, your transcript, no matter how impressive, will not help. Your lack of intellectual curiosity will quickly be discerned in an interview with a foreign firm, and you will not get the job.

Corporations that have made educational benefits available to their employees for many years have found, more often than not, that these benefits are not used because people "don't have the time" to go to school. Don't let this be your excuse—keep learning and growing!

## Work Experience

Generally, people don't have much difficulty listing the jobs they have held. It is important, however, to take each job apart and list all of your activities, including committees you may have served on, temporary assignments, and so on. All of these things may have relevance as you put your portfolio together.

Volunteer work and internships may be overlooked because they are unpaid. Don't fall into this trap! If you did something, whether you were paid or not, it has experiential value.

Volunteering can also acquaint you with the nuts and bolts of a field that you may want to enter. If you decide the field is for you, you already have people with whom you have worked who will write reference letters for you. These letters can greatly enhance your chances for gaining acceptance into schools, training programs, and entry-level positions.

## Other Activities

Teach classes, write articles for newspapers (even small neighborhood weeklies), and volunteer to serve on committees. All of these activities afford you an opportunity to build your body of knowledge and make your name better known to people who may be in a position to help you.

Even if you are happy where you are, review your portfolio on a regular basis and match your experience with the criteria listed in attractive classified ads. This is a risk-free activity that will enable you to address your shortcomings before they can cost you a job—including your present one!

The portfolio is useful as you prepare to write cover letters and tailor your resume for specific jobs. It's also useful for reviewing your career prior to interviewing for a new position. Now that you have the tools, take the time and make the effort to produce a winning portfolio of your own.

Past successes, academic or otherwise, are no guarantee that you will succeed in a new setting—no matter where you received your training.

For example, a linguist I know was on a translating assignment in Eastern Europe when he came across a graduate of one of our leading universities. This individual, who was also an attorney, wanted to charge clients an enormous amount of money to negotiate contracts for them in Russia. There was only one problem—he didn't really speak the language!

Yes, he had "studied" it, but he had received what used to be called "Gentlemen's Cs," meaning that he went through school without really being forced to learn anything. He applied English rules to Russian words and made no attempt to change tenses. He simply shoehorned Russian words into English-based sentences. The people with whom he came in contact were offended, and he was unable to do any business.

Yet, if you looked at his resume, he appeared to be qualified. After all, he had "studied" Russian at a first-rate university. But even if his Russian had been superb, he had never negotiated with someone in Russia. His client would have to pay while he learned how to do so. Many fine students tend to overlook the fact that, until you accumulate some on-the-job experience, you are of minimal value to a client or an employer.

Gwen Lawton, a senior human resources executive, never ceases to be amazed at the graduates of various business schools who, while still fanning the ink dry on their diplomas, inquire about senior positions and put their expected salary in the mid to upper range of the national average.

"They may have a B.S. in finance from a very fine school," she said, "and they may have served a summer internship with a large bank, which is also very good. However, the position they feel they are qualified for is already filled by someone who has a Ph.D. and twenty years' experience, and who is making less money than the student's expecting!" Gwen added that when entry-level jobs are offered to promising applicants, they frequently reject them and go off to search for "something better."

Face the facts: the world of work is largely a buyer's market. No one owes you a job, and in most cases, other resumes, many of them from highly experienced people, will be considered along with yours. Happily, many employers will take a chance on a comparative neophyte who shows potential, provided that applicant's approach is realistic.

### Determining Your Needs

One key to landing the best possible position is to undertake a thorough assessment of your monetary requirements. Because we all have unique needs based on our personal circumstances, I have purposely refrained from putting salary ranges in this book. That is because they are only averages, and are much too broad to address specific situations. What matters most is how appealing the job itself is to you and if it meets your financial and personal needs.

In order to determine what you need to make, take the time to put a budget together. Include the following:

- Food
- Housing
- Clothing
- Transportation
- Entertainment
- Continuing education
- Insurance

- Savings
- Utilities
- Credit cards and other debt service
- Other (emergency cash, day care, support for aging parents, and charitable contributions)

You also need to budget your time. Will the career you're considering afford you sufficient free time to have a life of your own outside of work?

The next step is to ask yourself if you are willing to relocate. If so, where are you willing to go? This is something you need to discuss with your significant others, since they will be impacted as well.

When researching prospective organizations, ask yourself whether or not the organization's values square with your own. If they do, and the working conditions are acceptable, you are well on your way to a successful arrangement. If they do not, you are likely to be unhappy eventually, no matter how much money you make.

## THE COVER LETTER

The cover letter is used to tie the company's want ad and your resume together. It stresses why you are a good applicant for this particular position. It points out things, such as relevant volunteer work, that may not be readily apparent when your resume is read.

The cover letter shows that you and the job are a superb match. A lot of thought needs to go into this because it's your best chance to arouse interest in you as a candidate. The goal at this point is not to secure the job, but to ensure they're convinced that you're someone whom they have to interview.

The career inventory we discussed earlier comes into play here, as it will help to provide you with maximum firepower as you write the letter.

Say why the position appeals to you and cite specific examples of experience and education that you believe make you a viable candidate. Be very positive and say that you are looking forward to learning more about the position.

## YOUR RESUME

Review the ad carefully. What exactly is the company looking for? How does your resume present you? Which items will need to be repositioned—and possibly reworded—to better match what the prospective employer is seeking? Keep in mind that we're talking about varying the presentation, not altering the facts.

Remember that promising resumes may be saved, so if you've applied to a given firm before, your previous resume may be on file, and it may end up being compared with your new one. It's no problem if they pretty well match up with each other—with allowances for different emphasis on certain items based on the job you were/are seeking—but if the two are wildly different, you will never get called for an interview.

## THE INTERVIEW PROCESS

You're likely to have multiple interviews. The first is a basic screening to see if you're as viable a candidate in real life as you appeared to be on paper. Later, if you have a successful first interview, you'll be called back to discuss in greater detail your qualifications—possibly with other members of the staff.

The interview requires significant preparation. Do your homework! Review your career and think through your answers to questions that you know the interviewer will ask.

Learn as much as you can about the organization in advance. Check out their website and, if possible, their annual report and advertising. Also devote time to learning about the organization's home country, even if the position you're applying for is in the United States.

Remember that a fairly common technique is to slide a manager into the receptionist's chair prior to an interviewee's arrival. This enables the firm to assess firsthand how you treat its employees. Remember, there is never a time when you aren't being evaluated. Even when it really is the receptionist behind the desk in the waiting area, he or she is frequently called in afterward to comment on the candidate's deportment.

The interview will have its own rhythm, and the interviewer will determine what that rhythm is. He or she will allow you numerous opportunities to display your skills, and it's important for you to listen very carefully and respond appropriately.

Be prepared for open-ended questions, such as the type that require detailed responses. "What aspects of your present position do you particularly enjoy, and why do you find them to be enjoyable?" is a popular question.

International screeners will likely probe deeply into your worldview and philosophy, and they're looking for serious responses. Steve Mulvihill, who, among other things, spent many years serving as the president of the U.S. affiliate of a European firm, says, "Humor and slang are always dangerous, because there's a good chance that you'll be taken seriously when you're joking, and the slang won't be understood, either." Speak sincerely when you are asked about personal beliefs.

In any interview, have legitimate questions of your own concerning the organization in general and the job in particular. It should be a learning experience on both sides. Hopefully, the interview will lead to more interviews and, ultimately, a job offer.

C H A P T E R

4

# HAS INTERNATIONAL BUSINESS EDUCATION CHANGED?

**U**pon completion of this chapter, you should be able to:

- Understand how the events of September 11 have affected the study of and interest in international business
- Speculate about the future of international business study and the unique considerations students must undertake post–September 11

Many people addressed the issue of changes in business in the wake of the attacks on the World Trade Center and the Pentagon. Among them was David J. Brennan, Ph.D., of Webster University in St. Louis, Missouri. Dr. Brennan is a world-class expert on international marketing and management. He delivered the following paper (which is reprinted with his permission) in March of 2002.

"Has international business education changed since September 11, 2001?" This question is not only difficult to answer but rivals that forever unanswerable "What is the meaning of life?" For the United States itself, the events of September 11, 2001, represent a faultline—a rude awakening—in American history. There is no doubt that America is now a different country, both at the macro and micro levels. There is uncertainty and personal fear, the stock markets are down and recession may be looming, but it remains to be seen how much of an effect it will have on international business and international business education.

In this paper, I take the position that some aspects of international business, and hence international business education, have changed while other aspects have not. At the same time, business, international business, and international business education are constantly changing and adapting to the world and the events—good, bad, and horrific—that happen. This paper addresses some of the academic and practical dimensions of international business. It takes a fairly narrow perspective in looking at possible direct impacts of recent events with respect to continued demand for international business education, implications for curriculum, impact on study and internships abroad, and perceptions of globalization.

## MARKET DEMAND

One of the basic considerations with respect to international business education following the tragic events is whether there will be continued demand for international business programs. I do not believe that there will be a significant decrease in international business education, but this issue needs to be addressed from three perspectives: needs of global business, educational institutions, and individual students. Global businesses will have a more immediate need for highly trained professionals who understand demanding and diverse international business tasks. As global business "speeds up" they will not be able to rely on excessive on-the-job training and will have a more immediate need for highly trained individuals who can "hit the ground running." Only comprehensive, high-level international business education can meet these needs. From the perspective of the international business educational institutions, universities and colleges will respond (or should respond) to the demands of the marketplace and global businesses. This response is in evidence today as graduate and undergraduate international business programs increase in numbers and enrollments. It is also evident in the increasing numbers of integrated programs—liberal arts international studies programs that include business/management courses—and an increased emphasis on international politics, languages, et cetera, in traditional business/management programs. From the perspective of the individual student there should be increased interest in international business education for two reasons. First, there will be an increased demand for a greater understanding of the world because the United States is no longer isolated as in the past. Second, future employment (and good salaries) will be available for well-trained international business professionals; they will follow the opportunities and the money. Thus, demand for international business education programs will likely continue to be high with support from many areas.

## CURRICULUM

The basic curriculum of international business programs will likely not change significantly. The core courses in management, accounting, economics, marketing, business law, et cetera, will remain to provide the necessary foundations. However, the areas of related disciplines—political and cultural aspects—will likely be emphasized more. Although the attacks on the United States were criminal, they were also political and cultural statements by the terrorists. It behooves international business students and their professors to seek and gain greater insights into why some groups would hate us and our way of life so much as to commit such an atrocity. There will be a greater need for American international business students to know and understand the important aspects of global politics and how these aspects are woven into international business activities. Greater cultural awareness and sensitivity are also necessary for the usually "sheltered" American student to better understand the management styles, customs, and motivations of not only foreign businesspeople, but also of the foreign markets and their consumers. The United States cannot continue to "export" our culture (products and services) blindly through American marketing efforts—even if the world seems to demand it—without realizing the potential for a possible "blowback" of negative impacts. Increasing emphasis on the study of foreign language (a window into a culture) and literature, plus a study of global relations would go a long way to opening the minds of international business students and allowing them a deeper understanding of the world and its peoples. It would also let them see how business, politics, and culture have become so interwoven today.

## STUDY ABROAD/INTERNATIONAL TRAVEL

The one area in which recent events may have a more direct and significant impact on international business education is in the increasing reluctance of American students to take study-abroad or foreign internship opportunities. These activities are key to a fully rounded international business education, as they provide exposure to foreign peoples and their cultures in "real time," not only in the primary area of the overseas classroom, but also in the secondary personal travel associated with studying and/or working abroad. My university is a global organization with several locations in Europe and Asia. Already, a decline in study-abroad applicants is noted, as well as the concern and distress of several students (and their parents) who are currently studying abroad. Although such opportunities are a personal choice, the mission of an international educational institution is to educate students as broadly and as completely as possible. As such, it has been decided that these opportunities will not be curtailed, but will be continued within reasonable bounds of security for the institution as well as for the students. A termination of such activities would deprive students of the very necessary and critical opportunity to live in a foreign culture, develop greater understanding of that culture, and obtain direct employment experience. These efforts need to be and must be continued and strengthened.

## GLOBALIZATION

Discussion of this topic would be incomplete without some comments on globalization. Globalization is the one reality today that can change many lives and change them positively forever. Fortunately, the good aspects of globalization—education, rising living standards, medicine, et cetera—far outweigh the bad aspects—environmental issues, cultural impacts, et cetera. The two sides of this phenomenon must be clearly differentiated and the positive emphasized. The terrorists themselves may be considered a creation of globalization as well as a strong, negative response to it. The developed nations' businesses need to see globalization in a new light. The increase in world trade, financial integration, the World Trade Organization, and regionalism (EU, NAFTA, et cetera) will neither stop nor likely even slow down. Perhaps globalization efforts should focus more on making it a "kinder and gentler" global movement, which will lessen its negative side. New perspectives from international business education, its professors, and students may assist.

# CONCLUSION

In conclusion, as the world has changed, so have international business and international business education changed. Hopefully, the changes will be positive and evolutionary, rather than revolutionary. Demand for international business education should remain strong. With regard to curriculum, an ever-increasing emphasis on the study of culture—language and religion—and global politics, and continuing emphasis on study abroad and foreign internship opportunities, will improve international business students' awareness and understanding of the world. These efforts can only enhance the more positive aspects of globalization.

C H A P T E R

5

# THREE MODES OF EMPLOYMENT

Upon completion of this chapter, you should be able to:

- Identify the differences between permanent and contract employment
- Determine which of the two you prefer
- Assess your potential for entrepreneurship or intrapreneurship
- Draft a business plan

## PERMANENT EMPLOYMENT

Many people feel more secure if they have permanent employment. That said, in an era of mergers, acquisitions, hostile takeovers and technological advances, no position is guaranteed for life, so it would benefit you to think like a consultant and look at your own company as a potential client. What services could you perform for them on a contract basis if you lost your job or decided to go into business for yourself? Have a plan for what you will be doing five or ten years down the road if you remain with your present employer, and have a backup plan if you suddenly get laid off.

Keep in mind that layoffs happen to good workers and managers, too. Often firms have to cut the payroll down to affordable size. Being laid off is no reflection on you as a person. The critical thing is to be ready, and to put your contingency plan to work as quickly as possible. The plan may well include contract work that you can do outside the office in your spare time or for your current employer, becoming what has sometimes been called an "intrapreneur."

### Intrapreneurship

Intrapreneurs are people who are able to convince their present employers to fund new ventures. They have to face the same obstacles as entrepreneurs, particularly when it comes to securing funding. Intrapreneurs, like entrepreneurs, may have to surrender a fairly high percentage of the profits in return for the money required to start the venture, but they are in a somewhat stronger position when it comes to hiring people.

Intrapreneurs jump through the same hoops as entrepreneurs when it comes to seeking funding (see the discussion later in this chapter). In the former case, you'll have the reputation of your existing company behind you, and you're likely to find it easier to hire the people you need. This may make it worth trading off a greater share of the profits than you'd receive as an entrepreneur because it increases the likelihood of there actually being profits.

This is a growing trend, as more and more firms are looking to outsource various functions. Your present employer may be a logical place to begin looking, and networking in the business community is also very helpful, as you may develop leads on firms that are open to this possibility. Vendors who serve your present employer may also be receptive to the idea. The key is to locate a firm that does a significant amount of international business and begin crafting your approach.

### Be Flexible

Free trade is coming, simply because it has to—it's just good business. So NAFTA, the WTO, and the like are gradually bringing us closer to a truly free and open global marketplace.

Thus, whatever you are doing, it is likely that the market will expand throughout the entire course of your career. It is imperative that you prepare for the inevitable changes so that you will not be left behind. An honest assessment of your current skills and the demands of the future is very much in order. If you are going to be rendered obsolete in the near term, make the requisite changes. Go back to school, learn a new set of skills, affiliate with a forward-looking organization—in short, do whatever it takes.

We are hard pressed to find a business day when the papers do not tell us of at least one major firm either going into bankruptcy or engaging in major "downsizing." Many of the layoffs are due to changes in the global marketplace.

One set of changes are the rapid-fire advancements in technology. While technological advances are a boon to manufacturers and consumers alike, they frequently mean the end of the (career) line for unskilled and semi-skilled workers and the managers who supervise them. Real people (not numbers) are suffering major upheaval in their lives because of these changes.

Be prepared for—and look forward to—a lifetime of continuous training in order to remain employable. In many cases, you will be vying for positions in direct competition with people from all over the world. Truly free trade means that individuals and organizations will all be "free" to succeed.

I remain optimistic about the future and the prospects for people who are willing to learn and grow are concerned. In short, if you are not afraid of change, and you are willing to keep studying so that your skills continue to grow, your future is likely to be a bright one.

You will work for and with people from all over the world. In the process, you will have an opportunity to test yourself not only in the commercial market, but also in the much more interesting marketplace of ideas.

## CONTRACT WORK

The distinction between contract and permanent employment really does not mean a lot any more. In the not-so-distant past, a regular position included a benefits package and, theoretically at least, a career path. Today, many organizations have cut back on benefits and have also reduced long-range opportunities because so many good people are available to work on a contract basis. Basically, as a contractor, you would become an independent vendor rather than an employee. There are certain legal requirements that concern the definition of a "contractor" under existing tax laws. You would be well advised to consult a tax specialist before embarking on this course of action so that you'll know up front what your income-reporting responsibilities are and what may be legitimately deducted as business expenses.

As long as your compensation under the contract allows you to comfortably pay for your own benefits package, this route can be a positive one. If you are good, more contracts will be forthcoming, with more flexibility and higher compensation. The following are some pros and cons for working on a contract basis:

1. Contract work is for a specified period.

**Con:** That means you are guaranteed employment only for a limited time.

**Pro:** Yes, and if you are good, the company will offer to renew the contract. And if you are really good, you will be free to sign a new, more lucrative contract elsewhere.

2. Contract work is limited in scope.

**Con:** You used to do a lot of things on the job. Now, the contract only calls for a few specific things.

**Pro:** These are the things you tend to do best. Now you are free to pursue these activities full-time, instead of having to drop them for, as your old job description said, "other duties as assigned."

3. Contract workers are not regular employees.

**Con:** You used to be part of the team; now you're an outsider.

**Pro:** When you were on the team, where were you on the organizational chart? Now you are a professional expert. The satisfaction of having one's work receive high priority cannot be overstated. Instead of being one of many among the permanent staff members, you are a pro and your time is worth money. Thus, you are able to do real work as a contract consultant, and it is infinitely preferable to downtime due to game-playing by those over you on the organizational chart.

## International Contract Work

Starting to drum up international contract work is as easy as looking around you. What needs doing? Start out with domestic clients and do a good job for them. The word will get out that you're affordable and talented.

Home is really the place to begin, as you know the territory, literally and figuratively. Network regularly and make it clear that you'd welcome foreign clients who need what you're already doing. For example, as Jesse Arman, a chartered financial consultant, says, "There is a niche for U.S.-based investment advisors and accountants who can provide foreign clients with useful information and services. . . . Simply put, an investment analysis prepared by a local national is likely to be more complete than one prepared by a counterpart in another country."

What's true of Mr. Arman's profession is true of others as well. What, precisely, do you bring to the party that would be of value to foreign clients? Spread the word! It's easy enough to do these days, thanks to our enhanced ability to contact people electronically all over the globe.

Your target firms are companies that are already doing at least a fair amount of international business or are planning to expand in the international sector. As a contractor, you're in a position to offer them the lower costs associated with not having to maintain a regular employee. Home in on the areas in which you're qualified to serve and contact the department heads. For example, if you're a cultural trainer, you'd want to query the head of the training department.

As a contractor, you'd present the distinct advantage of providing the firm with an as-needed service, custom-tailored to meet its needs. This would enable the firm to use its existing personnel—who might otherwise be pressed into service doing the tasks you're proposing to take over—to do the things that they were actually hired to do. This means that instead of being perceived as a threat to someone's job, you're a helpful specialist. As a result, you'll be considered a member of the team.

Generally speaking, the larger the firm, the more likely it is to be amenable to contractors. However, you may also be able to find prospects in progressive small companies that are able to determine how to prioritize their employees' activities. Simply put, although someone in a given firm may be qualified to do what you'd be doing as a contractor, the company may well be better served if that person devoted his or her time and energy to other activities. If you do a good job, you're likely to be on your way to a mutually beneficial, long-term relationship.

## STARTING YOUR OWN BUSINESS

Entrepreneurs take risks; most new businesses fail. Starting a new business is not for everyone because there are no guarantees that a going concern will be the end result—no matter how hard the people involved work. If the marketplace fails to show sufficient interest, the business dies.

The stress scares off most people, but thankfully there are still some hardy souls who are willing to put themselves on the line and bring new products and services to the market. If it were not for people like them, little or no economic progress would be made.

Venture capitalists, bankers, and corporations who are willing to put up money have one basic question: "What guarantees can you provide that you will pay us back on time and at an acceptable rate of return?" This is a fair question, as it is, after all, their money. They will grill you and thoroughly examine your business plan. Even if they are very interested, they may demand additional information, including a more fleshed-out plan. This will require time, money, and effort on your part (not to mention emotional "capital.") If you're unhappy with this, use your own money.

People who can run their own businesses have a great deal of determination and staying power. They are not deterred by setbacks, and they have prepared themselves financially to make the attempt to start and grow a business.

Can you deal with the stress of running your own business? Keep in mind that you are going to have to do more work than you have ever done before, particularly during the start-up phase. Evenings, weekends, and even holidays may find you working away—often performing tasks that could have been done more productively by others, if only you had sufficient cash flow to be able to hire them.

You may work for years and never make a cent. In addition to working for little or no pay, you may lose your own money directly by pouring it into the business, and indirectly by not being available for paying positions with other organizations. To be blunt: the odds are against you.

If the foregoing discourages you to the point of deciding against entrepreneurship, you have avoided the hardships involved. If it does not, you have the makings of an entrepreneur, and it is time to get to work!

## Preparing a Business Plan

A business plan is a must, and in addition to being a basic requirement for getting capital, it is a helpful exercise for you. It forces you to evaluate your ideas objectively and to determine in advance just how much time and effort are required. Here's a fairly standard model for a business plan's table of contents:

Executive Summary
Company Background
Company Products
Customer Base
Industry Background
Marketing Strategies
Management
Financial History
Financial Projections

Herbert C. Cohen, who provided the foregoing, has spent many years in publishing and has written a considerable number of successful business plans. Cohen says, "Rest assured that everyone will read the table of contents and the executive summary, just to be sure that everything's there. After that, they tend to read only the parts that are within their areas of expertise."

Cohen's points are well taken. The decision to lend or not to lend is usually made by a committee, and not everyone is going to read your entire plan. Therefore it is important for each section to be complete enough to stand on its own.

Let's walk through the plan, which may be titled "Confidential Investment Summary," item by item.

### Executive Summary

This is an abridged version of your entire plan. It encapsulates the main features of the plan. Your readers want an overview here, one that hits the highlights and gives them a good general picture of what you intend to do. It must grab the reader, and it should not run more than two or three pages at most.

### Company Background

If yours is an existing company, and you are seeking the money to go international, provide a history of your firm. If not, what led to bringing this proposed venture into being?

### Company Products

Again, if you have some history, go over it here. What have you done in the past? What kind of returns have you paid investors that funded your other products? If this is totally new, why have you decided to provide this particular product? (Note: your product may be a service.)

### Customer Base

Who will buy your product? How many of them are there? Where are they located? In the case of exporting, where do you intend to sell the product overseas? How will it be distributed? By whom? What are the laws and regulations you will need to comply with? What are your prospective customers' current purchasing options; in other words, what else is on the market? What will provide you with a competitive edge? Also, what is going on with your customers' local economy? Do they have the ability to purchase your product? To them, is it a luxury or a necessity?

### Industry Background

Who are your competitors? This was touched upon briefly in the previous section, but go into detail here. Will you be a major innovator, a "me too" provider (offering something at a significant discount), or have you created something no one else has, designed to penetrate and capture a small segment of the market that will not be lucrative enough to attract competition but will allow you to make an acceptable profit?

### Marketing Strategies

How will you make your potential customers aware of what your product is, what it will do for them, how much it costs, and where they can get it? (Note: to complete this section, you will have to produce a detailed marketing plan.)

### Management

This section provides your managers' resumes in narrative form, similar to what you'd find in a baseball yearbook or a theatre program. Hit the high points: Who are your key players? What skills do they bring to the venture? What are their educational backgrounds? What awards have they won? What are their greatest achievements? What, specifically, will they be doing to implement this business plan? (Note: standard resumes should also appear in your appendices, along with other material to support your claims.)

### Financial History

How well have you and your management team handled money in the past, either with your present firm or elsewhere? Indicate the rates of return you have earned for people who have put up money for plans you have created and implemented.

### Financial Projections

Typically, financial projections should be carried out for a three- to five-year period. Find out in advance what the people you are trying to raise money from want to see.

Generally, people who write business plans tend to be unduly optimistic and ask for less money than they actually need. This may lead to the plan's being rejected out of hand for being unrealistic. Or, while you may get the money you asked for, you'll be caught in the embarrassing (and frequently impossible) position of attempting to raise more money in midstream. In this case, you will probably have to pay a lot more for the additional money than you can ultimately afford, because investors will know that you are desperate. Most new businesses fail due to under-capitalization, literally and figuratively—don't get cut short!

Feel free to list the risks involved. This is a good exercise for you because it will let you know what you're up against. You will also strike potential investors as someone who thinks things through and has the confidence (and the plan) to overcome adversity.

Your plan should be understandable and concise. A good approach is to employ a strategy discussed elsewhere in this book—pretend you are writing a telegram that is going to cost you $50 a word.

Management consultant Berle Larned suggests knocking out a draft of your plan as quickly as possible. Put it aside for a few days. Then go back and fill in the blanks.

At this point, you may find that you'll need outside help from marketing and financial experts. Once you have your final draft, says Larned, show it to someone who has no stake in it. (You may want to have them sign a confidentiality agreement first.) If they can understand it, you're on the right track.

## Taking Your Business Global

The U.S. Department of Commerce can provide a great deal of help to budding international entrepreneurs. They're in the government pages of the phone book, and they're also on the Web. Get in touch with them early on in the planning process and go back with questions as often as you need to.

In addition, the following three tips may help get your creative juices flowing when it comes to brainstorming new, viable products in the international market:

1. Wearables and collectibles that are obviously from the United States do very well in overseas markets.
2. Thanks to a wonderful instrument called the letter of credit (ask an international banker), overseas collections are often easier than domestic ones.
3. You don't have to be a big firm to do well in the international marketplace—all you need is a viable product or service.

These days, many small firms are leading the way when it comes to creating cutting-edge technologies and other new ways of doing business. They've found a niche for themselves, and that same opportunity is there for you!

C H A P T E R

6

# CAREERS IN INTERNATIONAL SALES AND MARKETING

**U**pon completion of this chapter, you should be able to:

- Understand what sales and marketing careers are and are not
- Assess your interest in these fields
- Evaluate your qualifications
- Prepare a plan for acquiring the tools you will need to pursue a sales or marketing career

Plunging directly into international sales may require specific qualifications. For example, I was able to steer one college senior who is fluent in Spanish and about to earn a degree in chemistry to a chemical manufacturer that was looking for a person to help cover a territory in Central America. His linguistic ability and degree made him someone they wanted to talk to. He's still going through the interviewing process as I write this, and he's being considered for an entry-level position in customer service, where he'll work with an experienced team. If he's hired, he'll help to service existing accounts and be groomed for advancement to a regular sales position.

In many cases, firms will require not only specific degrees and linguistic ability before hiring someone to sell in the international sector, but also a proven track record in the domestic sales arena. In-person sales calls are a costly proposition in the domestic marketplace—and those costs are considerably higher in international business—so their demands are not unreasonable considering that they'll make a significant investment in anyone they hire.

## SALES CAREERS

*Sales* is not a dirty word! Frequently, positions advertised under the heading of "Marketing" in the classifieds are actually sales positions. A person's business card may read "Marketing Representative," but if that person is not selling, he or she will not be employed for long. Sales has had a negative connotation for many years, and we still laugh at archetypes like the door-to-door sales reps who plague Dagwood and other comic-strip characters. These "salesmen," who are pushing worthless products, literally stick a foot in the door and will not take no for an answer. In reality, today's salespeople are not this colorful. They are professionals whose main task is to help their customers.

### What Salespeople Do

The bulk of selling, outside of telemarketing and retailing, is performed on a business-to-business basis. Men and women who succeed in this profession are, first of all, good listeners. Listening is the key to the selling process because your prospective customers will, if you let them, tell you what you need to know to clinch the deal. Let's start at the beginning.

A prospect is someone who has a potential need for your product, has the funds to pay for it (through his or her company), and has the authority to make the buying decision. *Cold calling* is contacting a prospect and scheduling an appointment for a presentation.

Your employer will have a list of prospective customers, but you are also expected to develop additional business. This means doing some prospecting on your own, particularly at trade shows and conventions.

In business-to-business selling, it is fairly easy to secure an appointment. There are a number of reasons for this. The first is that part of your prospect's job is to keep current with the state-of-the-art products and services designed to help his or her organization do a better job. Second, it is helpful to prospects to know the representative for an alternative source, and finally, even if they are completely happy with their present vendor, it doesn't hurt for them to let their regular representative know that they have been talking with you. That way, the prospects ensure that they will not be taken for granted by their current vendor.

Once you have the appointment, it is time to prepare for it. Your homework begins with learning everything you can about the prospect's organization. Have they purchased from your firm in the past? If so, and they no longer do, what led to losing their business? Do they currently purchase from another division of your company? If so, how is that relationship going? What are their future plans? A look at their website and annual report can be most helpful in this regard, as are industry- and function-specific publications and websites, which will keep you abreast of changing trends.

Which of your products lend themselves to the prospect's needs? Once you have determined this, bone up on the critical features of the products, with an emphasis on the specific benefits they will provide to this particular prospect.

Be aware of the prospect's product and shopping alternatives. In short, know and respect your competitors. After all, they have market share, which means that they are doing at least some things right. Keep in mind, however, that it does not pay to criticize your competitors—they are in the same business you are, so tearing them down is, by extension, putting your own organization down.

When you are selling internationally, either in the United States or overseas, a legitimate question a prospective client may ask is how you intend to service their account: what will you do if something goes wrong? Anticipate this question, because the answer to it may determine whether your sales proposal will be considered.

If you are a contract representative for one or more firms, you should already have determined how much business you can legitimately handle. This is a valid concern for the firms you represent as well as for prospective customers because if you are spread too thin, your efforts for everyone will be insufficient.

Years ago, Victor Kiam of Remington (the electric shaver manufacturer) looked at sales in the Japanese market. At that point, his company was represented in Japan by an organization whose salespeople serviced a variety of accounts in addition to Remington.

Mr. Kiam arranged for a small sales organization to come into being in Japan, one that would devote all of its efforts to selling his firm's products. Not surprisingly, this resulted in a very significant increase in sales.

Keep in mind that what you are selling—provided that your firm's products can meet your prospect's needs—is, very often, yourself. Sales reps work with their customers and help to facilitate the manufacturing and distribution processes in order to meet the customers' needs and deadlines.

Salespeople also help in the new product development process—they report what the competition is doing and relay customers' desires for new products.

If you are a conscientious problem-solver and know what you are selling and its best applications, chances are that you will be able to overcome resistance, particularly when it comes to price, and get the order. As a salesperson, you work with the customer and provide value-added service to that customer (above and beyond the product itself) that can result in a cost-justification purchase, even if your company charges more than your competitors. Before a sales call, look at every possible objection a prospective customer may raise and have satisfactory answers prepared in advance.

### The Call Itself

An old-timer once told me to be sure that I read the local paper each morning before I went out on sales calls. He said, "That way, you'll know what's going on that's of importance in the prospect's community, and you'll have some good opening conversational gambits."

In the international sector, it is of particular importance to know what can and cannot be discussed with someone from a given culture. Even if you're using an interpreter, be very careful which topics you choose and, to play it safe, do not use humor, as many jokes do not translate well. Further, as Bob Wing, a longtime international sales and marketing professional adds, "There's a good chance that you'll be considered to be a frivolous person, and that can hurt your chances of getting the order." So, while there may be a bit of small talk while you are settling in, pay attention to what you're saying. Be pleasant, but not overly familiar.

Overcoming objections is something you will do a lot of during a sales call. The two most common objections are that the prospect's organization does not have the money to pay for your product and, even if they did, it's too expensive anyway.

If what you are offering is going to help them do a better job and thereby end up saving them money, the funding can be arranged somewhere in the organization. Contingency budgets exist for this very purpose. Further, if you truly are a value-added representative, you're giving them more "bang for the buck."

Keep in mind that you will be tested frequently by prospects. They want to know if you are going to be there for the long haul. This is particularly true in the international sector.

In the old days, sales executives would say, "Don't take 'no' for an answer!" They would also complain if you "left money on the table," which meant, in their minds, that you did not sell everything you could have. Today, it is understood that there are legitimate reasons for saying no, and that, rather than overselling now (talking them into purchasing something they really don't need) and losing the customer forever, you build gradually and develop an ongoing relationship. In the long term, this will make more money for your company. Legitimate reasons for saying no include the following:

1. They really don't have the money now, and they have been told to hold the line on expenses.
2. They have recently purchased something similar from the competition, and it would be impolitic to replace it now.
3. They have no history with you and your firm, so they aren't sure of your staying power.
4. A major change in the firm's composition is pending (merger, takeover, et cetera), and their people have been told to refrain from purchasing anything new so that they can maximize profits by cutting short-term costs.

A "no" doesn't mean that you give up. As a sales manager I know told me, "We want to penetrate new markets, so I've told our reps to contact prospects regularly, even though they aren't ordering from us. Over a period of time, it will occur to them that they hear from us more often than they do the people whom they're buying from. In other words, our competitors are taking them for granted. At that point, we'll start doing business."

Long-term relationships are the norm in the international sector, so persistence is definitely a virtue.

### Closing the Deal

The close is something that happens again and again during a sales call. Your first close will come very early on in your presentation when you state why you are there. After an objection has been raised and you have satisfied the prospect with your answer, close (ask for the order) again. Do this each time you handle an objection. Finally, at the end of the presentation, ask for the order again. After all, that is why you are there.

Follow up with phone calls, E-mails, and letters as appropriate. Personalize them to the greatest extent possible, but within culturally acceptable boundaries. If a prospect is interested in a particular activity and you see an article on it in a newspaper or magazine, cut it out and send it to him or her along with a note. This helps solidify the fact that you see the prospect as an individual and appreciate him or her for who they are. It opens a lot of doors and makes the business relationship a lot more pleasant.

## Characteristics of Successful Salespeople

The real pros bounce back from hearing negative responses because they do not take rejections (and there are a lot of them) personally. They learn from each encounter, reshape their presentations, and keep on plugging away.

They also aren't desperate. They are willing to spend whatever time it takes to eventually win a prospect over. Desperation shows! If you are up against a wall and your job is on the line, your nonverbal communication will be a dead giveaway, and the prospect will back off.

Professionals do not oversell. Their main function is to help the customer determine needs and to match products and services so that the needs are satisfied. Through sheer force of personality you may be able to sell someone something they don't really need. Once. This will provide a short-term gain for you, but it is an example of winning the battle but losing the war. The customer will quickly come to resent what you did, and new orders will be a long time coming, if indeed they ever do business with you again.

Business-to-business selling is a profession. Unlike part-time sales, such as real estate—where some "dabblers" may sell a house or two a year and let it go at that—in business-to-business selling you are on call all the time. There is a great deal of pressure to produce because there are plenty of people who want your job. Solid professionals are not frightened by competition, they welcome it. Can you handle this kind of pressure?

A sales job is not for everyone, and the fact that you have sold one type of product does not mean you can sell all things. Each sales situation is somewhat different, and that is even more the case in international sales, either here or abroad.

## Preparing to Enter a Career in Sales

The place to start in sales is with a domestic position, one that will enable you to gain experience and assess your long-term potential.

Begin by checking the classifieds for sales positions. Do not accept one prematurely. After all, there is a tremendous amount of turnover in entry-level sales positions. This is because most new salespeople are unable to earn enough to pay for their basic expenses while they are attempting to establish themselves. Wait until you're financially ready to take the plunge. Consider using an employment agency in addition to or instead of answering classified ads (including those on the Web). The agency representatives, once they know what you're looking for, can set up worthwhile interviews for you. In order for this to happen, you will need to answer the following questions:

- What types of products or services would you feel comfortable selling?
- Are you willing to travel? If so, how far and how often?
- Are you willing to relocate? If so, immediately, or after a probationary period that helps you to determine if you are

comfortable with the company and the job? Also, if relocation is an acceptable option, are you prepared to make the move? How about your lease or mortgage? What about your personal life, including your significant others? Does the company pay relocation expenses? Will it help you to pay off your lease or sell your home? If you require this sort of assurance up front, tell the agency. That way, they will not send you to a firm that can't meet your needs.

- Are you willing to pay part or all of the employment fee for the job? Employment agencies make their money by providing qualified applicants to their clients. The agencies perform a valuable screening service, and the payoff comes when someone they've sent to a company is actually hired. Please note that a lot of firms will be willing to reimburse you for at least a portion of the fee if you work out, and many companies will pay the fee themselves. The important issue here is that if you are not willing to pay any fee, ever, you should let them know up front. That way, you're not wasting anyone's time because you will not be interviewed for those positions.

## Qualifications Needed for Sales Positions

Some sales jobs have very specific requirements, including holding a particular degree. Obviously, if you're in the technical realm, this is understandable. Other types of sales jobs are open to people with general backgrounds, and a degree may be desirable, but not required. Here are some areas of study that are helpful:

Marketing
Psychology
Public speaking
Communications: interpersonal and small group dynamics
Languages

It goes without saying that you must like to and be able to work with people in all kinds of settings in order to succeed in sales. This includes one-on-one and both small and large groups.

## Travel

Many sales positions, even domestic ones, require travel. Even if your territory is in a major metropolitan area, you can still count on a fair amount of travel to sales meetings, trade shows, and conventions. If you cover a large territory, you will spend a lot of time on the road, driving and flying.

While the idea of travel sounds glamorous, it really isn't all about seeing exotic new lands. More likely, you'll be on your feet for hours at a time at trade shows and conventions, followed by putting in time at your company's hospitality suites. At mealtimes, you're expected to entertain clients while convincing them to buy from you. In addition, most salespeople spend a great deal of time on their own, which has certain pluses. On the other hand, it means your immediate social support system will often be far away. If you are involved in international selling, covering your territory will likely require extended periods of time away from home.

In their book *International Marketing* (McGraw-Hill, 2002), Philip Cateora and John Graham sum it all up on page 522:

> International sales is hard work. A typical week for this Canadian executive looks like this: Leaves Singapore with the flu. Arrives home in Toronto to discover that a frozen pipe has burst. Immediately boards a plane for a two-day trip to Chicago. Back to Toronto. On to Detroit, battling jet lag and the flu. Back to Toronto, running through the Detroit airport . . . and throwing his briefcase into a closing door. Takes a brief break in his flooded house before boarding another plane to China. Reports having woken up in a plane and asking his seatmate where they were landing. Seventeen flights in two weeks has left him a bit confused.

## Compensation

Compensation for sales representatives varies, as do the methods of payment. For example, some firms pay on a straight commission basis. This scares many people, who ask, "But what if I don't sell anything?" The answer to that is that if you don't sell anything, your compensation is a moot point because you won't be working there very long.

Good sales reps generally prefer commissions because it makes the amount of money they earn a product of their own initiative, rather than settling for a fixed amount. If you have something in reserve to support you while you are establishing yourself in a sales career, commissions can wait. Generally, people who are embarking upon a second career and have money coming in (such as retired military) can handle the start-up phase long enough to determine if they are cut out for sales. If you are not prepared for this, look for firms that will pay a draw against future commissions or provide a stipend for a short period while you are getting on your feet.

Salaries plus commission is another possibility, but this is generally for fields that require a longer gestation period for orders to be placed. During that time, you will be working extensively with customers, helping to shape the right combination of products and services to meet their needs. Selling oil field equipment and supplies is a good example of this because, even on the same patch, every hole is different.

There are also variations of the foregoing, such as straight salary or salary with bonuses. The critical question before accepting any sales position is: are you financially secure enough to give yourself an honest chance of succeeding on the job?

## MARKETING CAREERS

Here, too, I advocate looking for work in the domestic sector prior to going international in order to gain valuable experience that will directly transfer to the international sector. Let's look at three areas within marketing: public relations, specialty advertising, and market research.

### Public Relations

"PR types" have traditionally been viewed askance by senior executives. Dubbed "spin doctors" until recently, they were called in to "fix" things whenever an organization was getting bad press.

But now, we've entered the era of integrated marketing, and more and more, the PR people are in at the very beginning, along with advertising and marketing personnel. PR professionals are also in a position to advise their employers before plans are finalized and put into motion.

PR specialists are responsible for promoting their clients in the media. News stories generally have a more favorable impact on the marketplace than advertisements because news items have an ascribed credibility, while ads are usually suspect.

Although you'll be expected to target the trade press (industry- and function-specific publications) as well as general-circulation newspapers and publications, don't overlook the opportunity to enhance the strength of your firm's website. This is particularly germane within the international sector, as many foreign firms' English-language sites need upgrading, in terms of content and style, in order to appeal to U.S. or Canadian readers.

Your tasks may include writing press releases (try to keep it to one page—pretend that you're sending a telegram at $50 a word—by confining yourself to *who*, *what*, *where*, and *when*), "ghostwriting" stories (or at least helping with the editing for budding authors within the organization), writing speeches, arranging events, and helping to facilitate internal contacts for outside reporters and photographers.

You will be expected to move seamlessly from one task to the next, meeting very tight deadlines, and you'll be held to very high performance standards in terms of generating positive press for your employer. Take, for example, the case of Maxine Whidden.

Maxine Whidden (not her real name) is now a very successful PR practitioner. In fact, she owns a successful agency. Years ago, though, she had no experience, and there were no entry-level jobs to be had.

Maxine belonged to a small classical music group that was a registered nonprofit entity. When the press promoted their concerts, they sold out most performances. Other times, when there was little or no publicity, the group lost money. The group's publicity chairperson said, "Sometimes they (papers, radio, and TV stations) run our stuff, sometimes they don't. I don't know why."

Maxine had an idea and volunteered for the publicity committee. One week later, she was "promoted" to chairperson. She made inquiries and discovered that her predecessor had been very careless when it came to meeting deadlines for community calendars and getting mentioned elsewhere in the press. Sometimes she was on time, often, she wasn't. Maxine vowed to change this.

Her discovery taught her that, when it comes to promotion, you're dealing with 2 percent creativity and 98 percent attention to detail—giving editors and reporters the *who*, *what*, *when*, and *where* in a timely manner.

Over time, she built up a reputation for dependability in this area and cultivated key contacts in the media. It was a relatively easy jump to go from writing to producing PSAs (Public Service Announcements) for radio and TV because they were based on her press releases and contained the same basic information. The stations were happy to give her free training in production, provided that she came in during slow periods.

Her friends in the media also provided her with tapes and clippings of her work, and she built a portfolio for herself—one that enabled her, after a time, to land a job in advertising. She was on her way.

The fact is, Maxine had prepared herself for the world of work. And, in the process, she was also able to help promote a group whose philosophy and goals she valued. Her blueprint can be readily adapted to meet your needs.

Find a nonprofit group that you believe in, one that needs help promoting itself. Once you've proven yourself as a PR person for the group, you'll be in a position to solicit contacts from within the group and from others in your personal network. In fact, if Maxine had not gotten the job with the agency, that's precisely what she would have done. Doing this will afford you the opportunity to try marketing without leaving your present job. If, after a fair trial, you decide it isn't for you, you're ahead of the game on two counts: first, you've made an informed decision regarding this type of career move, and second, you've really helped a group you believe in.

## Specialty Advertising

Chances are that you are wearing, carrying, or using something produced by the specialty advertising industry. It may be a sweatshirt, coffee mug, calendar, key chain, or one of thousands of other items that carry a corporate or organizational logo or advertising message.

These items are frequently used as giveaways after sales presentations or at trade shows and conventions. They may also be premiums that you receive when you purchase a product, such as a lighter attached to a carton of cigarettes.

The specialty advertiser's goal is to provide you with something that you will use, look at (and others who come into your orbit will see it, too), and eventually, heed the message.

Ray Morgan is prominent in this industry, and he is constantly coming up with new items for his customers. His challenge is to provide something that will exert a positive influence on everyone who comes in contact with it. Having done that once, he is expected to continue producing winners; the pressure is really on because there is a lot of competition in this field.

Of course, there are also a lot of opportunities, and you are most likely going to break in as a commission-only rep. This is something you can try on your own, either on a part-time basis or on behalf of an organization you belong to.

For example, years ago, Ray helped a church increase its Sunday attendance by having "Let God Straighten Out Your Life" printed on a pencil that looked like a pretzel. Along with the snappy one-liner was the church's name, address, and times of services. This was used as a giveaway to potential parishioners, and it achieved the desired effect.

Certain items could be used as fundraisers, and by coordinating this with a specialty advertising firm, you can test the waters to see if you'd like to do this sort of thing for a living. Specialty advertising is a hybrid field, as it involves both sales and marketing skills, and it is no place for the timid.

Ray advocates studying marketing throughout your career. He continuously reads textbooks, attends lectures, and audits college courses. He says, "The day that I think I've learned all I need to know about marketing is the day I'm on my way out the door, because I will have set myself up for a fall."

The marketplace is constantly evolving, and it requires ongoing monitoring and study to stay ahead of the curve. This is the fascinating challenge that keeps people like Ray Morgan plugging away.

## Market Research

Market research is something you will do a lot of, even though your job title may not reflect it. Product managers, marketing managers, and salespeople all conduct a great deal of market research; they are constantly meeting with existing and potential customers and finding out what they want.

The process begins when you discover that you need to learn something about their product and shopping alternatives.

Once you have determined what you need to find out, you decide who knows this information and choose the best ways to contact them. These methods may include any or all of the following:

- Focus groups
- Direct mail (including E-mail)
- Telephone surveys
- Personal interviews (including scheduled appointments, door-to-door cold calling, and mall intercepts)

Many entry-level marketing research positions are part-time, and the pay is usually low. However, jobs are always available, the basic education requirements for most entry-level positions are minimal, and you can gain a great deal of experience in a short time.

The key to conducting market research is to be neutral and not let your own biases creep into the proceedings. What matters are the opinions of the people you are querying, not yours.

A part-time job with a market research firm or an ad agency that conducts research will quickly teach you how the process works. You're likely to start out doing mall intercepts or making phone calls. Either way, you'll soon be able to answer the following questions:

- Can you remain neutral and yet enthusiastic about the surveys?
- Are you able to talk with very different types of people?
- Can you make your quotas?
- Is this what you want to do every day?

Several months of part-time work will tell you if you should develop your skill sets through more formal training, such as courses in marketing, research techniques, communications, and languages.

During the trial period, you will also be able to test your selling skills, as there will be times when you have a quota to meet, time is running out, and the person you are talking to needs to be convinced that their opinion is important and that completing the interview is a worthwhile endeavor for them.

Once you've determined that this type of work is something you'd like to pursue at a higher level, it's time to begin the search for your next job. Your present employer is a good place to begin, but if it doesn't have a desirable career path, check the classifieds regularly and work with an employment agency or two.

Sales and marketing careers are challenging. If you can handle the pressure, however, any of the careers in sales and marketing we have looked at can be very rewarding. Good people are always in demand and thanks to a high turnover, entry-level positions are frequently there for the taking. Once you have established yourself in the domestic marketplace, you are ready to look at the international sector.

# TEACHING ENGLISH ABROAD

**U**pon completion of this chapter, you should be able to:

- Assess the pros and cons of teaching overseas
- Take steps to determine if you are cut out for teaching

Thus far in this book, I've stressed the importance of pursuing knowledge throughout your lifetime in order to have a broad base of knowledge and interests, which will help you succeed in overseas work. This will enable you to interact with and excel in foreign countries and with people of diverse interests and backgrounds.

One of the best ways to get a solid understanding of a culture and its people is by living and working in the country itself. That said, it may be difficult when you have little or no experience working internationally to make the jump from the domestic business sector to the international one. One stepping-stone to your career in international business might be teaching English abroad.

These positions can provide you with many valuable experiences that will make you a more desirable employee down the road in the corporate sector. In addition to the new skills you bring to an employer, you'll benefit from living and working in a particular country and likely become familiar with the business opportunities available there.

# "WANT TO WORK OVERSEAS? TEACH ENGLISH!"

The ads make it look deceptively simple—all you have to do is use your native language skills to teach English to people in foreign lands. Generally speaking, if you have a degree in any discipline and are interested in working with people, overseas schools are, according to many ads, ready to put you to work.

In fact, jobs do abound in this area and they offer a variety of cultural, educational, and monetary experiences. Because of this, you should do thorough research into the program that's of interest to you because the quality of your working and living conditions may vary enormously. In addition, you should know whether or not you are cut out to be a teacher. Let's look at what's involved.

First of all, the majority of worthwhile positions require some form of certification. Here are some common ones:

TESOL: Teacher of English to Speakers of Other Languages
CELTA: Certificate of English Language Teaching to Adults
CELTC: Certificate of English Language Training to Children
TEFL: Teaching English as a Foreign Language

There are plenty of schools in the United States and Canada willing to train you as a teacher, and the courses they offer last from a few weeks to several months. The best place to find information concerning such schools and the job market for teachers is in *Transitions Abroad* magazine (transitionsabroad.com), and in a book put out by them called *Work Abroad*. This useful volume is updated regularly and doesn't gloss over potential problems you may encounter when you're living and working overseas. It also contains inside information from people who truly know the territory in countries that are looking for teachers, volunteers, and people to work for pay in a variety of fields. Generally speaking, the information contained in *Work Abroad* has appeared earlier in the magazine.

Keep in mind that teaching abroad, while it may be a stepping-stone to your career in international business, is also a profession and not something to be entered into lightly. Various articles in *Transitions Abroad* have stressed the importance of getting your teaching certificate(s) from schools whose graduates are readily hired. In short, any school can produce its own certificate; the key question is, what is the certificate's value in the international marketplace?

Certificate courses in the United States and Canada can easily run into thousands of dollars, with room, board, and travel costs adding to your up-front expenditures. These expenses are likely to be higher if you opt to study overseas.

One thing is vital, no matter where you study: the course should require that you spend time actually teaching in a supervised environment. The fact is, not everyone is cut out to be a teacher, and it's better to learn up front if you're likely to do well.

You may also consider doing volunteer work in your own community by tutoring people who are learning English. Doing so will afford you the opportunity to learn if teaching's something you're good at and something you would actually enjoy doing for a living. If possible, work with both children and adults to test your comfort level with both groups.

You might also run an ad in a nearby college or university's newspaper, indicating your availability to tutor foreign students for an hourly fee. Ask around to determine the going rate. The paper itself may contain ads requesting conversation partners, or the school's office for foreign students may be able to put you in touch with one or more people who need to practice their English.

The key is to determine your own comfort level before spending large sums of money to prepare for something you may not be suited for. If, after working for several months, either for pay or as a volunteer, you conclude that you're interested in pursuing this further, it will be time to start shopping for schools.

## ADDITIONAL CONSIDERATIONS

It's important to determine if you're actually able to teach (many very intelligent people aren't), and teaching actually appeals to you. (I've known people who are "naturals" who have tried it and quickly burned out.) When determining whether or not you'll be a successful teacher abroad, keep in mind the following critical considerations:

- What's your comfort level with various age groups? Your answer will determine where you might or might not fit in.
- Where would you like to live and work? Your ideal place may have a glut of experienced teachers already in place.
- What's "Plan B?" Very often, teachers are offered a contract for an academic year, which means you'll have to factor in several unpaid months.
- What will you do during this time off? Teaching English abroad can be a great adventure for a single person or a couple who is willing and able to teach. But it's frequently difficult to pay the bills for two (or more) if only one of you has a regular teaching contract.
- What are your financial obligations back home? Do you have car and credit card payments? A mortgage? If you're renting, where will you live when you return? Your teaching salary may allow you to live well on the local economy in some countries, but will it give you enough to cover all of your expenses, including those you may retain at home?
- Does your position offer health benefits or will you have to provide them on your own? In addition, keep in mind that your annual salary while overseas is unlikely to be augmented by a 401K or other form of retirement plan, as you're usually only an adjunct faculty member.

## MEET AN EXPERT

Lisa Hammond taught English in Japan, China, and France. These days, she teaches people in the United States who want to teach English as a second language (ESL).

*What was your educational background, particularly in terms of foreign languages, when you decided to try teaching English abroad?*

Initially, I had a B.A. in political science and no background or experience in teaching English. I studied Spanish from junior high school through college and some basic French in high school and college, as well. In short, aside from being a native English speaker, I had no special qualifications for my first teaching job in Japan.

### *Does it help a prospective ESL teacher to know how to speak at least one foreign language? Why?*

I believe it is important for a prospective ESL/EFL teacher to have some experience with a second language. In very practical terms (basic survival skills and everyday interactions), my background in Spanish and French was not directly beneficial to my living in Japan. However, in terms of teaching English, my experience in studying other languages was valuable. It provided me with a notion of how languages work, a starting point for how I might approach my own teaching, and familiarity with specific grammatical terms used in a language classroom.

### *How did you go about choosing your countries and applying for your teaching positions?*

When I first became interested in teaching English abroad, I was most interested in working in Europe, particularly Spain or France. I went to the library and looked through all of the books on finding an overseas job and tracked down the names and addresses of various schools, colleges, and language programs. I sent out dozens of letters and resumes. I got absolutely no response. It became apparent to me rather quickly that without a degree in TESOL or any teaching experience, my opportunities for employment were rather remote. Applying for jobs from the United States, rather than being there in person to make inquiries and submit applications, made it additionally difficult. I then refocused my efforts on Japan, where teaching positions were more plentiful and schools seemed more willing to hire and provide a work visa and paid transportation to applicants from the United States. I ended up utilizing a Japanese friend who hand-delivered my resume to a specialized language college in Sendai, Japan, and personally recommended me as an English teacher. Since personal connections are extremely important in Japan, I believe this was the primary reason I was hired for my first teaching job abroad.

After I completed my M.A. in TESOL, I decided I wanted to teach over-seas again. I was interested in returning to Asia and had heard a lot of very positive information about teaching in China. At that time, there were many opportunities for qualified English teachers (officially termed "Foreign Experts") in China, so I went ahead and applied directly to three different language institutes. I received three job offers.

My third experience was quite different. My husband and I had relocated to Toulouse, France, for his employment. My particular visa did not permit me to look for work, so finding a job was difficult. At one point, I heard about a private high school that was looking for a part-time English teacher. I called the school, had a brief interview, and was hired. In exchange for my teaching, the school paid the tuition for the French classes I was taking at the time.

## What surprised you about your experiences in each country?

I have encountered many surprises during my time spent living and working abroad. In Japan, I was most unprepared for the widespread xenophobia I encountered. Even though I lived in a fairly sizeable city, for many of my college students, I was the first Westerner they had actually met in person. Some admitted to being petrified of my blue eyes. Outside of work, there was a considerable amount of gawking and pointing at me when I walked down the street. At first it was somewhat fun to feel like a minor celebrity. Then it became extremely annoying and engendered a great deal of anger on my part. I finally grew to accept this as a part of my daily life in Japan and it became less irritating. On a more positive note, it takes a very long time for a person in Japan (especially a foreigner) to be considered a "friend." But, once a friend, you are a friend for life. Nearly fifteen years after leaving the country, my Japanese friends have proven to be some of the most consistent and faithful friends I've ever had.

In China, I taught at a language institute in Beijing that was associated with the machine-building industry. My students were all adults, ranging from their early twenties to late fifties. The vast majority of them had grown up during the Cultural Revolution. Schools were closed down during that time and many people were sent to the countryside for re-education through labor. My students sometimes discussed their feelings about never having had a real childhood. One result of being products of the Cultural Revolution was my students' complete and utter reverence for learning. They proved to be some of the most eager and appreciative students I have ever encountered. Another, more surprising, consequence of this was their totally childlike behavior at times. On one occasion we took a class trip to a famous park in Beijing. There happened to be a dodge-car ride in the park, which these students rode with great delight. Afterward, I must have mentioned how surprised I was that they would enjoy such an activity. One student explained that they were now making up for a part of their missed childhoods.

I can't say that there were any major surprises about my living and teaching in France. I can say that the longstanding stereotype of the French as being quite stuffy and rude, especially to foreigners, was contrary to my personal experience. The French people whom I encountered were—without exception—friendly, kind, and helpful.

### *What was your readjustment to life in the U.S. like when you returned?*

My return from China was extremely difficult and emotional. I taught in Beijing from June 1989 to August 1998, and I was there during the pro-democracy movement. I was at Tiananmen Square with a number of my students on June 5th, the night the army opened fire on the demonstrators. I had left earlier in the evening, but most of my students remained at the Square. As a result of the shootings and at the very strong urging of the American Embassy, all the American and other foreign instructors from my institute, and most others throughout Beijing, left China within two or three days. It was a hastily arranged departure. We left without saying any goodbyes and without knowing if our students were still alive. We took only what we could reasonably carry and placed our trust in the institute that our belongings would be shipped to us. Upon returning home, there were constant reports on the news about the large numbers of people killed and arrested as part of the government's crackdown. It was agonizing to watch and listen to these reports. It was not actually until many months later that I finally learned that all of my students had been able to leave Tiananmen Square that night and were safe.

My return to the United States after living in France was the least problematic. While our overall experience of living in France was very positive and enjoyable, both my husband and I found our employment situations to be disappointing. After one year, we returned to the States and readjusted to our new lives here with minimal difficulty.

*It's trite, but true, that not everyone is cut out to teach English or live abroad. That said, what's an "ideal" prospective teacher like?*

I believe that an "ideal" prospective teacher would be a person who is flexible, adaptable, creative, and open-minded. These qualities are important to being an effective teacher, but even more important in terms of being able to deal with the stresses, strains, and ups and downs of living in a foreign country and culture.

*Can the overseas teaching experience lead to work in the corporate world? How?*

Yes. There are limited opportunities in teaching English for corporations that deal with international employees. This is usually done on a contract basis. Additionally, some former teachers have found employment in the area of cross-cultural training for corporations that send employees overseas or hire international employees in the United States.

*What advice would you give to someone who is thinking of following your example?*

Maybe not to follow my particular example! I would strongly encourage anyone interested in teaching English to get some training before going abroad. There are short-term, intensive TESL certificate programs that provide basic training in teaching ESL/EFL. If that is not feasible, visit ESL programs in the community (at adult education centers, some colleges and universities, and in conjunction with volunteer programs) to get some exposure. There is a wide variety of books available that can be helpful in getting started. While it is possible to find employment without any educational background or experience in TESOL, the more education, training, and experience one has in the field, the more employment options will be available.

## ONE LAST NOTE

As a native English speaker and teacher, you're in a position to circumvent the usual barriers put up to keep foreign workers out of many countries. The people whom I've known who have done this for years revel in living abroad and are willing to make whatever sacrifices it takes to make the opportunity work. The key is to know right up front what's required of you and determine if you're a good candidate. Good luck and safe travels!

# C H A P T E R  8

# AN INTRODUCTION TO BASIC RESUME AND COVER LETTER WRITING

**U**pon completion of this chapter, you should be able to:

- Be familiar with the elements of an effective resume
- Identify your skills, talents, and experience and be able to position these in a resume or cover letter
- Understand the difference between a chronological and functional resume

Now that you've explored the field of international business and understand the educational and work requirements necessary to enter into the field, the next step is to effectively pitch yourself to your prospective employer with a great resume and cover letter. While some people find this to be a daunting task, it doesn't have to be. Through careful consideration and the advice in this chapter, writing a resume that makes you stand out from the rest should be a fairly painless task.

Your resume is a piece of paper (or an electronic document) that serves to introduce you to the people who will eventually hire you. To write a thoughtful resume, you must thoroughly assess your personality, your accomplishments, and the skills you have acquired. The act of composing and submitting a resume also requires you to carefully consider the company or individual that might hire you. What are they looking for, and how can you meet their needs? This chapter will show you how to organize your personal information and experience into a concise and well-written resume, so that your qualifications and potential as an employee will be understood easily and quickly by a complete stranger.

Writing the resume is just one step in what can be a daunting job-search process, but it is an important element in the chain of events that will lead you to your new position. While you are probably a talented, bright, and charming person, your resume may not reflect these qualities. A poorly written resume can get you nowhere; a well-written resume can land you an interview and potentially a job. A good resume can even lead the interviewer to ask you questions that will allow you to talk about your strengths and highlight the skills you can bring to a prospective employer. Even a person with very little experience can find a good job if he or she is assisted by a thoughtful and polished resume.

Lengthy, typewritten resumes are a thing of the past. Today, employers do not have the time or the patience for verbose documents; they look for tightly composed, straightforward, action-based resumes. Although a one-page resume is the norm, a two-page resume may be warranted if you have had extensive job experience or have changed careers and truly need the space to properly position yourself. If, after careful editing, you still need more than one page to present yourself, it's acceptable to use a second page. A crowded resume that's hard to read would be the worst of your choices.

Distilling your work experience, education, and interests into such a small space requires preparation and thought. This chapter takes you step-by-step through the process of crafting an effective resume that will stand out in today's competitive marketplace.

## THE ELEMENTS OF AN EFFECTIVE RESUME

An effective resume is composed of information that employers are most interested in knowing about a prospective job applicant. This information is conveyed by a few essential elements. The following is a list of elements that are found in most resumes—some essential, some optional. Later in this chapter, we will further examine the role of each of these elements in the makeup of your resume.

- Heading
- Objective and/or Keyword Section
- Work Experience
- Education
- Honors
- Activities
- Certificates and Licenses
- Publications
- Professional Memberships
- Special Skills
- Personal Information
- References

The first step in preparing your resume is to gather information about yourself and your past accomplishments. Later you will refine this information, rewrite it using effective language, and organize it into an attractive layout. But first, let's take a look at each of these important elements individually so you can judge their appropriateness for your resume.

## Heading

Although the heading may seem to be the simplest section of your resume, be careful not to take it lightly. It is the first section your prospective employer will see, and it contains the information she or he will need to contact you. At the very least, the heading must contain your name, your home address, and, of course, a phone number where you can be reached easily.

In today's high-tech world, many of us have multiple ways that we can be contacted. You may list your E-mail address if you are reasonably sure the employer makes use of this form of communication. Keep in mind, however, that others may have access to your E-mail messages if you send them from an account provided by your current company. If this is a concern, do not list your work E-mail address on your resume. If you are able to take calls at your current place of business, you should include your work number, because most employers will attempt to contact you during typical business hours.

If you have voice mail or a reliable answering machine at home or at work, list its number in the heading and make sure your greeting is professional and clear. Always include at least one phone number in your heading, even if it is a temporary number, where a prospective employer can leave a message.

You might have a dozen different ways to be contacted, but you do not need to list all of them. Confine your numbers or addresses to those that are the easiest for the prospective employer to use and the simplest for you to retrieve.

## Objective

When seeking a specific career path, it is important to list a job or career objective on your resume. This statement helps employers know the direction you see yourself taking, so they can determine whether your goals are in line with those of their organization and the position available. Normally, an objective is one to two sentences long. Its contents will vary depending on your career field, goals, and personality. The objective can be specific or general, but it should always be to the point.

If you are planning to use this resume online, or you suspect your potential employer is likely to scan your resume, you will want to include a "keyword" in the objective. This allows a prospective employer, searching hundreds of resumes for a specific skill or position objective, to locate the keyword and find your resume. In essence, a keyword is what's "hot" in your particular field at a given time. It's a buzzword, a shorthand way of getting a particular message across at a glance. For example, if you are a lawyer, your objective might state your desire to work in the area of corporate litigation. In this case, someone searching for the keyword "corporate litigation" will pull up your resume and know that you want to plan, research, and present cases at trial on behalf of the corporation. If your objective states that you "desire a challenging position in systems design," the keyword is "systems design," an industry-specific, shorthand way of saying that you want to be involved in assessing the need for, acquiring, and implementing high-technology systems. These are keywords and every industry has them, so it's becoming more and more important to include a few in your resume. (You may need to conduct additional research to make sure you know what keywords are most likely to be used in your desired industry, profession, or situation.)

There are many resume and job-search sites online. Like most things in the online world, they vary a great deal in quality. Use your discretion. If you plan to apply for jobs online or advertise your availability this way, you will want to design a scannable resume. This type of resume uses a format that can be easily scanned into a computer and added to a database. Scanning allows a prospective employer to use keywords to quickly review each applicant's experience and skills, and (in the event that there are many candidates for the job) to keep your resume for future reference.

Many people find that it is worthwhile to create two or more versions of their basic resume. You may want an intricately designed resume on high-quality paper to mail or hand out *and* a resume that is designed to be scanned into a computer and saved on a database or an online job site. You can even create a resume in ASCII text to E-mail to prospective employers. For further information, you may wish to refer to the *Guide to Internet Job Searching*, by Frances Roehm and Margaret Dikel, updated and published every other year by VGM Career Books, a division of the McGraw-Hill Companies. This excellent book contains helpful and detailed information about formatting a resume for Internet use. To get you started, I have included a list of things to keep in mind when creating electronic resumes.

Although it is usually a good idea to include an objective, in some cases this element is not necessary. The goal of the objective statement is to provide the employer with an idea of where you see yourself going in the field. However, if you are uncertain of the exact nature of the job you seek, including an objective that is too specific could result in your not being considered for a host of perfectly acceptable positions. If you decide not to use an objective heading in your resume, you should definitely incorporate the information that would be conveyed in the objective into your cover letter.

## Work Experience

Work experience is arguably the most important element of them all. Unless you are a recent graduate or former homemaker with little or no relevant work experience, your current and former positions will provide the central focus of the resume. You will want this section to be as complete and carefully constructed as possible. By thoroughly examining your work experience, you can get to the heart of your accomplishments and present them in a way that demonstrates and highlights your qualifications.

If you are just entering the workforce, your resume will probably focus on your education, but you should also include information on your part-time or volunteer experiences. Although you will have less information about work experience than a person who has held multiple positions or is advanced in his or her career, the amount of information is not what is most important in this section. How the information is presented and what it says about you as a worker and a person is what really counts.

As you create this section of your resume, remember the need for accuracy. Include all the necessary information about each of your jobs, including your job title, dates of employment, name of your employer, city, state, responsibilities, special projects you handled, and accomplishments. Be sure to list only accomplishments for which you were directly responsible. And don't be alarmed if you haven't participated in or worked on special projects, because this section may not be relevant to certain jobs.

The most common way to list your work experience is in *reverse chrono-logical order*. In other words, start with your most recent job and work your way backward. This way, your prospective employer sees your current (and often most important) position before considering your past employment. Your most recent position, if it's the most important in terms of responsi-bilities and relevance to the job for which you are applying, should also be the one that includes the most information as compared to your previous positions.

Even if the work itself seems unrelated to your proposed career path, you should list any job or experience that will help "sell" your talents. If you were promoted or given greater responsibilities or commendations, be sure to mention the fact.

## Education

Education is usually the second most important element of a resume. Your educational background is often a deciding factor in an employer's deci-sion to interview you. Highlight your accomplishments in school as much as you did those accomplishments at work. If you are looking for your first professional job, your education or life experience will be your greatest asset because your related work experience will be minimal. In this case, the education section becomes an important means of selling yourself.

Include in this section all the degrees or certificates you have received; your major or area of concentration; all of the honors you earned; and any relevant activities you participated in, organized, or chaired. Again, list your most recent schooling first. If you have completed graduate-level work, begin with that and work your way back through your undergraduate education. If you have completed college, you generally should not list your high school experience; do so only if you earned special honors, you had a grade point average that was much better than the norm, or this was your highest level of education.

If you have completed a large number of credit hours in a subject that may be relevant to the position you are seeking, but did not obtain a degree, you may wish to list the hours or classes you completed. Keep in mind, however, that you may be asked to explain why you did not finish the program. If you are currently in school, list the degree, certificate, or license you expect to obtain and the projected date of completion.

## Honors

If you include an honors section in your resume, you should highlight any awards, honors, or memberships in honorary societies that you have received. (You may also incorporate this information into your education section.) Often, the honors are academic in nature, but this section also may be used for special achievements in sports, clubs, or other school activities. Always include the name of the organization awarding the honor and the date(s) received.

## Activities

Perhaps you have been active in different organizations or clubs; often an employer will look at such involvement as evidence of initiative, dedication, and good social skills. Examples of your ability to take a leading role in a group should be included on a resume, if you can provide them. The activities section of your resume should present neighborhood and community activities, volunteer positions, and so forth. In general, you may want to avoid listing any organization whose name indicates the race, creed, sex, age, marital status, sexual orientation, or nation of origin of its members because this could expose you to discrimination.

## Certificates and Licenses

If your chosen career path requires specialized training, you may already have certificates or licenses. You should list these if the job you are seeking requires them and you, of course, have acquired them. If you have applied for a license but have not yet received it, use the phrase "application pending."

License requirements vary by state. If you have moved or are planning to relocate to another state, check with that state's board or licensing agency for all licensing requirements.

Always make sure that all of the information you list is completely accurate. Locate copies of your certificates and licenses, and check the exact date and name of the accrediting agency.

## Publications

Some professions strongly encourage or even require that you publish. If you have written, coauthored, or edited any books, articles, professional papers, or works of a similar nature that pertain to your field, you will definitely want to include this element. Remember to list the date of publication and the publisher's name, and specify whether you were the sole author or a coauthor. Book, magazine, or journal titles are generally italicized, while the titles of articles within a larger publication appear in quotes. (Check with your reference librarian for more about the appropriate way to present this information.) For scientific or research papers, you will need to give the date, place, and audience to whom the paper was presented.

## Professional Memberships

Another potential element in your resume is a section listing professional memberships. Use this section to describe your involvement in professional associations, unions, and similar organizations. It is to your advantage to list any professional memberships that pertain to the job you are seeking. Many employers see your membership as representative of your desire to stay up-to-date and connected in your field. Include the dates of your involvement and whether you took part in any special activities or held any offices within the organization.

## Special Skills

The special skills section of your resume is the place to mention any special abilities you have that relate to the job you are seeking. You can use this element to present certain talents or experiences that are not necessarily a part of your education or work experience. Common examples include fluency in a foreign language, extensive travel abroad, or knowledge of a particular computer application. "Special skills" can encompass a wide range of talents, and this section can be used creatively. However, for each skill you list, you should be able to describe how it would be a direct asset in the type of work you're seeking because employers may ask just that in an interview. If you can't think of a way to do this, it may be extraneous information.

## Personal Information

Some people include personal information on their resumes. This is generally not recommended, but you might wish to include it if you think that something in your personal life, such as a hobby or talent, has some bearing on the position you are seeking. This type of information is often referred to at the beginning of an interview, when it may be used as an "icebreaker." Of course, personal information regarding your age, marital status, race, religion, or sexual orientation should never appear on your resume as *personal information*. It should be given only in the context of memberships and activities, and only when doing so would not expose you to discrimination.

## References

References are not usually given on the resume itself, but a prospective employer needs to know that you have references who may be contacted if necessary. All you need to include is a single sentence at the end of the resume: "References are available upon request," or even simply, "References available." Have a reference list ready—your interviewer may ask to see it! Contact each person on the list ahead of time to see whether it is all right for you to use him or her as a reference. This way, the person has a chance to think about what to say *before* the call occurs. This helps ensure that you will obtain the best reference possible.

## WRITING YOUR RESUME

Now that you have gathered the information for each section of your resume, it's time to write it out in a way that will get the attention of the reviewer—hopefully, your future employer! The language you use in your resume will affect its success, so you must be careful and conscientious. Translate the facts you have gathered into the active, precise language of resume writing. You will be aiming for a resume that keeps the reader's interest and highlights your accomplishments in a concise and effective way.

Resume writing is unlike any other form of writing. Your seventh-grade composition teacher would not approve, but the rules of punctuation and sentence building are often completely ignored. Instead, you should try for a functional, direct writing style that focuses on the use of verbs and other words that imply action on your part. Writing with action words and strong verbs characterizes you to potential employers as an energetic, active person, someone who completes tasks and achieves results from his or her work. Resumes that do not make use of action words can sound passive and stale. These resumes are not effective and do not get the attention of any employer, no matter how qualified the applicant. Choose words that display your strengths and demonstrate your initiative. The following list of commonly used verbs will help you create a strong resume:

| | |
|---|---|
| administered | built |
| advised | carried out |
| analyzed | channeled |
| arranged | collected |
| assembled | communicated |
| assumed responsibility | compiled |
| billed | completed |

conducted

contacted

contracted

coordinated

counseled

created

cut

designed

determined

developed

directed

dispatched

distributed

documented

edited

established

expanded

functioned as

gathered

handled

hired

implemented

improved

inspected

interviewed

introduced

invented

maintained

managed

met with

motivated

negotiated

operated

orchestrated

ordered

organized

oversaw

performed

planned

prepared

presented

produced

programmed

published

purchased

recommended

recorded

reduced

referred

represented

researched

reviewed

saved

screened

served as

served on

sold

suggested

supervised

taught

tested

trained

typed

wrote

Let's look at two examples that differ only in their writing style. The first resume section is ineffective because it does not use action words to accent the applicant's work experiences.

**Regional Sales Manager**

Manager of sales representatives from seven states. Manager of twelve food chain accounts in the East. In charge of the sales force's planned selling toward specific goals. Supervisor and trainer of new sales representatives. Consulting for customers in the areas of inventory management and quality control.

**Special Projects:** Coordinator and sponsor of annual food-industry sales seminar.

**Accomplishments:** Monthly regional volume went up 25 percent during my tenure while, at the same time, a proper sales/cost ratio was maintained. Customer-company relations were improved.

In the following paragraph, we have rewritten the same section using action words. Notice how the tone has changed. It now sounds stronger and more active. This person accomplished goals and really *did* things.

**Regional Sales Manager**

Managed sales representatives from seven states. Oversaw twelve food chain accounts in the eastern United States. Directed the sales force in planned selling toward specific goals. Supervised and trained new sales representatives. Counseled customers in the areas of inventory management and quality control. Coordinated and sponsored the annual Food Industry Seminar. Increased monthly regional volume 25 percent and helped to improve customer-company relations during my tenure.

One helpful way to construct the work experience section is to make use of your actual job descriptions—the written duties and expectations your employers had for a person in your current or former position. Job descriptions are rarely written in proper resume language, so you will have to rework them, but they do include much of the information necessary to create this section of your resume. If you have access to job descriptions for your former positions, you can use the details of these to construct an action-oriented paragraph. Often, your human resources department can provide a job description for your current position.

The following is an example of a typical human resources job description, followed by a rewritten version of the same description employing action words and specific details about the job. Again, pay attention to the style of writing instead of the content, as the details of your own experience will be unique.

**Public Administrator I**
**Responsibilities:** Coordinate and direct public services to meet the needs of the nation, state, or community. Analyze problems; work with special committees and public agencies; recommend solutions to governing bodies.
**Aptitudes and Skills:** Ability to relate to and communicate with people; solve complex problems through analysis; plan, organize, and implement policies and programs. Knowledge of political systems, financial management, personnel administration, program evaluation, and organizational theory.

**Public Administrator I**
Wrote pamphlets and conducted discussion groups to inform citizens of legislative processes and consumer issues. Organized and supervised 25 interviewers. Trained interviewers in effective communication skills.

After you have written out your resume, you are ready to begin the next important step: assembly and layout.

## ASSEMBLY AND LAYOUT

At this point, you've gathered all the necessary information for your resume and rewritten it in language that will impress your potential employers. Your next step is to assemble the sections in a logical order and lay them out on the page neatly and attractively to achieve the desired effect: getting the interview.

### Assembly

The order of the elements in a resume makes a difference in its overall effect. Clearly, you would not want to bury your name and address somewhere in the middle of the resume. Nor would you want to lead with a less important section, such as special skills. Put the elements in an order that stresses your most important accomplishments and the things that will be most appealing to your potential employer. For example, if you are new to the workforce, you will want the reviewer to read about your education and life skills before any part-time jobs you may have held for short durations. On the other hand, if you have been gainfully employed for several years and currently hold an important position in your company, you should list your work accomplishments ahead of your educational information, which has become less pertinent with time.

Certain things should always be included in your resume, but others are optional. The following list shows you which are which. You might want to use it as a checklist to be certain that you have included all of the necessary information.

| **Essential** | **Optional** |
|---|---|
| Name | Cellular Phone Number |
| Address | Pager Number |
| Phone Number | E-Mail Address or Website Address |
| Work Experience | Voice Mail Number |
| Education | Job Objective |
| References Phrase | Honors |
| | Special Skills |
| | Publications |
| | Professional Memberships |
| | Activities |
| | Certificates and Licenses |
| | Personal Information |
| | Graphics |
| | Photograph |

Your choice of optional sections depends on your own background and employment needs. Always use information that will put you in a favorable light—unless it's absolutely essential, avoid anything that will prompt the interviewer to ask questions about your weaknesses or something else that could be unflattering. Make sure your information is accurate and truthful. If your honors are impressive, include them in the resume. If your activities in school demonstrate talents that are necessary for the job you are seeking, allow space for a section on activities. Each resume is unique, just as each person is unique.

## Types of Resumes

So far we have focused on the most common type of resume—the *reverse chronological* resume—in which your most recent job is listed first. This is the type of resume usually preferred by those who have to read a large number of resumes, and it is by far the most popular and widely circulated. However, this style of presentation may not be the most effective way to highlight *your* skills and accomplishments.

For example, if you are reentering the workforce after many years or are trying to change career fields, the *functional* resume may work best. This type of resume puts the focus on your achievements instead of the sequence of your work history. In the functional resume, your experience is presented through your general accomplishments and the skills you have developed in your working life.

A functional resume is assembled from the same information you have already gathered. The main difference lies in how you organize the information. Essentially, the work experience section is divided in two, with your job duties and accomplishments constituting one section and your employers' names, cities, and states; your positions; and the dates employed making up the other. Place the first section near the top of your resume, just below your job objective (if used), and call it *Accomplishments* or *Achievements*. The second section, containing the bare essentials of your work history, should come after the accomplishments section and can be called *Employment History*, since it is a chronological overview of your former jobs.

The other sections of your resume remain the same. The work experience section is the only one affected in the functional format. By placing the section that focuses on your achievements at the beginning, you draw attention to these achievements. This puts less emphasis on whom you worked for and when, and more on what you did and what you are capable of doing.

If you are changing careers, the emphasis on skills and achievements is important. The identities of previous employers (who aren't part of your new career field) need to be downplayed. A functional resume can help accomplish this task. If you are reentering the workforce after a long absence, a functional resume is the obvious choice. And if you lack full-time work experience, you will need to draw attention away from this fact and put the focus on your skills and abilities. You may need to highlight your volunteer activities and part-time work. Education may also play a more important role in your resume.

The type of resume that is right for you will depend on your personal circumstances. It may be helpful to create both types and then compare them. Which one presents you in the best light?

### Special Tips for Electronic Resumes

Because there are many details to consider in writing a resume that will be posted or transmitted on the Internet, or one that will be scanned into a computer when it is received, we suggest that you refer to the *Guide to Internet Job Searching*, by Frances Roehm and Margaret Dikel, as previously mentioned. However, here are some brief, general guidelines to follow if you expect your resume to be scanned into a computer.

- Use standard fonts in which none of the letters touch.
- Keep in mind that underlining, italics, and fancy scripts may not scan well.
- Use boldface and capitalization to set off elements. Again, make sure letters don't touch. Leave at least a quarter inch between lines of type.
- Keep information and elements at the left margin. Centering, columns, and even indenting may change when the resume is optically scanned.
- Do not use any lines, boxes, or graphics.
- Place the most important information at the top of the first page. If you use two pages, put "Page 1 of 2" at the bottom of the first page and put your name and "Page 2 of 2" at the top of the second page.
- List each telephone number on its own line in the header.
- Use multiple keywords or synonyms for what you do to make sure your qualifications will be picked up if a prospective employer is

searching for them. Use nouns that are keywords for your profession.

- Be descriptive in your titles. For example, don't just use "assistant"; use "legal office assistant."
- Make sure the contrast between print and paper is good. Use a high-quality laser printer and white or very light-colored 8½-by-11-inch paper.
- Mail a high-quality laser print or an excellent copy. Do not fold or use staples, as this might interfere with scanning. You may, however, use paper clips.

In addition to creating a resume that works well for scanning, you may want to have a resume that can be E-mailed to reviewers. Because you may not know what word processing application the recipient uses, the best format to use is ASCII text. (ASCII stands for "American Standard Code for Information Exchange.") It allows people with very different software platforms to exchange and understand information. (E-mail operates on this principle.) ASCII is a simple, text-only language, which means you can include only simple text. There can be no use of boldface, italics, or even paragraph indentations.

To create an ASCII resume, just use your normal word processing program; when finished, save it as a "text only" document. You will find this option under the "save" or "save as" command. Here is a list of things to *avoid* when crafting your electronic resume:

- Tabs. Use your space bar. Tabs will not work.
- Any special characters, such as mathematical symbols.
- Word wrap. Use hard returns (the return key) to make line breaks.
- Centering or other formatting. Align everything at the left margin.
- Bold or italic fonts. Everything will be converted to plain text when you save the file as a "text only" document.

Check carefully for any mistakes before you save the document as a text file. Spellcheck and proofread it several times; then ask someone with a keen eye to go over it again for you. Remember: the key is to keep it simple. Any attempt to make this resume pretty or decorative may result in a resume that is confusing and hard to read. After you have saved the document, you can cut and paste it into an E-mail or onto a website.

## Layout for a Paper Resume

A great deal of care—and much more formatting—is necessary to achieve an attractive layout for your paper resume. There is no single appropriate layout that applies to every resume, but there are a few basic rules to follow in putting your resume on paper:

- Leave a comfortable margin on the sides, top, and bottom of the page (usually one to one and a half inches).
- Use appropriate spacing between the sections (two to three line spaces are usually adequate).
- Be consistent in the *type* of headings you use for different sections of your resume. For example, if you capitalize the heading EMPLOYMENT HISTORY, don't use initial capitals and underlining for a section of equal importance, such as <u>Education</u>.
- Do not use more than one font in your resume. Stay consistent by choosing a font that is fairly standard and easy to read, and don't change it for different sections. Beware of the tendency to try to make your resume original by choosing fancy type styles; your resume may end up looking unprofessional instead of creative. Unless you are in a very creative and artistic field, you should almost always stick with tried-and-true type styles like Times New Roman and Palatino, which are often used in business writing. In the area of resume styles, conservative is usually the best way to go.
- Always try to fit your resume on one page. If you are having trouble with this, you may be trying to say too much. Edit out any repetitive or unnecessary information, and shorten descriptions of earlier jobs where possible. Ask a friend you trust for feedback on what seems unnecessary or unimportant. For example, you may have included too many optional sections. Today, with the prevalence of the personal computer as a tool, there is no excuse for a poorly laid-out resume. Experiment with variations until you are pleased with the result.

## BARRY GOODNIGHT
118 21st Place • Jackson Beach, CA 90266
213-555-3815 • barrygoodnight@xxx.com

Seasoned sales and marketing competitor with well-developed instincts for what will sell. Strong record of success with channel marketing and system level sales in North America and international markets. Accomplished in managing sales teams and indirect sales forces. Effective in utilizing analytical skills to organize marketing plans, sales strategies, and resolution of marketing resource issues at the executive level.

1999 to Present
Director of International Marketing
Lackland Technology Corporation

Directed North American and international sales in Japan, Mexico, and South America for fault-tolerant client server in corporate MIS departments. Defined market and sales strategies that accounted for 50 percent of corporate revenues.

Defined economic market size and available market for fault-tolerant client server in corporate MIS departments in North America. Directed the sale of $2 million in hardware components during the first 60-day promotional rollout.

Developed and implemented sales plans and channel pricing strategies to boost North American sales.

Managed and structured channel communication program and developed a direct sales program to banks and other financial institutions.

1988 to 1999
Marketing and Sales Manager
Trecor Manufacturing, Inc.

Managed the overall sales for a $225 million division engaged in the development of telecommunications systems.

Directed a national field sales and marketing program for a new product line that resulted in identification of $30 million in new sales opportunities.

Evaluated the feasibility of developing international alliances to improve market penetration into the Pacific Rim countries.

**100**
CAREERS IN
INTERNATIONAL
BUSINESS

Barry Goodnight
Page 2 of 2

1979 to 1988
Territory Sales Representative
Inman Heavy Equipment

Marketed the company's construction-related products in a five-state region.

Successfully opened 35 new accounts in the previously untested Oregon marketplace.

Education

B.A. Economics, Cornell University, 1969

Awarded Arthur Finkin National Scholarship

Additional Information

Eagle Scout; active in coaching boys' baseball.

References available upon request.

Irwin C. Savage
123 Glendale Dr.
Mt. Auburn, MA 01111
617-555-6876

## Objective

A position in international trade that would utilize my background in import/export and my knowledge of the French and German languages.

## Accomplishments

- Responsible for more than $2 million in new sales of French-made construction equipment to U.S.-based home manufacturers.

- Negotiated a free-trade agreement between the top 27 French building manufacturers.

- Coordinated the introduction of German-manufactured synthetic plywood products into the U.S. marketplace.

- Negotiated transshipping rates as an alternative to airborne traffic, resulting in savings of $100,000.

- Recruited and hired an overseas sales staff of 10. Sales team consistently exceeded marketing objectives by 21 to 45 percent.

- Received the "Order of Excellence" award from the British Department of Economic Incentives in recognition of my work in fostering an environment of economic support between the United States and Great Britain.

- Entered the U.S. Army following graduation with honors from West Point as a second lieutenant.

- Promoted through the ranks and retired honorably as a lieutenant colonel in 1995.

## Employment History

Auckland International Distributors, Senior Sales Agent–1995 to present

United States Army, retired lieutenant colonel–1975 to 1995

## Education

United States Army Academy, West Point, NY

B.A., Engineering, 1975

Remember that a resume is not an autobiography. Too much information will only get in the way. The more compact your resume, the easier it will be to review. If a person who is swamped with resumes looks at yours, catches the main points, and then calls you for an interview to fill in some of the details, your resume has already accomplished its task. A clear and concise resume makes for a happy reader and a good impression.

There are times when, despite extensive editing, the resume simply cannot fit on one page. In this case, the resume should be laid out on two pages in such a way that neither clarity nor appearance is compromised. Each page of a two-page resume should be marked clearly: the first should indicate "Page 1 of 2," and the second should include your name and the page number, for example, "Julia Ramirez—Page 2 of 2." The pages should then be stapled together. You may use a smaller font (in the same font as the body of your resume) for the page numbers. Place them at the bottom of page one and the top of page two. Again, spend the time now to experiment with the layout until you find one that looks good to you.

Always show your final layout to other people and ask them what they like or dislike about it, and what impresses them most when they read your resume. Make sure that their responses are the same as what you want to elicit from your prospective employer. If they aren't the same, you should continue to make changes until the necessary information has been emphasized.

## Proofreading

After you have finished typing the master copy of your resume and before you have it copied or printed, thoroughly check it for typing and spelling errors. Do not place all your trust in your computer's spellcheck function. Use an old editing trick and read the whole resume backward—start at the end and read it right to left and bottom to top. This can help you see the small errors or inconsistencies that are easy to overlook. Take time to do it right because a single error on a document this important can cause the reader to judge your attention to detail in a harsh light.

Have several people look at the finished resume just in case you've missed an error. Don't try to take a shortcut; not having an unbiased set of eyes examine your resume now could mean embarrassment later. Even experienced editors can easily overlook their own errors. Be thorough and conscientious with your proofreading so your first impression is a perfect one.

We have included the following rules of capitalization and punctuation to assist you in the final stage of creating your resume. Remember that resumes often require use of a shorthand style of writing that may include sentences without periods and other stylistic choices that break the standard rules of grammar. Be consistent in each section, and throughout the whole resume, with your choices.

### Rules of Capitalization

- Capitalize proper nouns, such as names of schools, colleges, and universities; names of companies; and brand names of products.
- Capitalize major words in the names and titles of books, tests, and articles that appear in the body of your resume.
- Capitalize words in major section headings of your resume.
- Do not capitalize words just because they seem important.
- When in doubt, consult a manual of style such as *Words into Type* (Prentice-Hall) or *The Chicago Manual of Style* (The University of Chicago Press). Your local library can help you locate these and other reference books. Many computer programs also have grammar help sections.

### Rules of Punctuation

- Use commas to separate words in a series.
- Use a semicolon to separate series of words that already include commas within the series. (For an example, see the first rule of capitalization.)
- Use a semicolon to separate independent clauses that are not joined by a conjunction.
- Use a period to end a sentence.
- Use a colon to show that examples or details follow that will expand or amplify the preceding phrase.
- Avoid the use of dashes.
- Avoid the use of brackets.
- If you use any punctuation in an unusual way in your resume, be consistent in its use.
- Whenever you are uncertain, consult a style manual.

### Putting Your Resume in Print

You will need to buy high-quality paper for your printer before you print your finished resume. Regular office paper is not good enough for resumes; the reviewer will probably think it looks flimsy and cheap. Go to an office supply store or copy shop and select a high-quality bond paper that will make a good first impression. Select colors like white, off-white, or possibly a light gray. In some industries, a pastel may be acceptable, but be sure the color and feel of the paper makes a subtle, positive statement about you. Nothing in the choice of paper should be loud or unprofessional.

If your computer printer does not reproduce your resume properly and produces smudged or stuttered type, either ask to borrow a friend's or take your disk (or a clean original) to a printer or copy shop for high-quality copying. If you anticipate needing a large number of copies, taking your resume to a copy shop or a printer is probably the best choice.

Hold a sheet of your unprinted bond paper up to the light. If it has a watermark, you will want to point this out to the person helping you with copies; the printing should be done so that the reader can read the print and see the watermark the right way up. Check each copy for smudges or streaks. This is the time to be a perfectionist—the results of your careful preparation will be well worth it.

## THE COVER LETTER

Once your resume has been assembled, laid out, and printed to your satisfaction, the next and final step before distribution is to write your cover letter. Though there may be instances where you deliver your resume in person, you will usually send it through the mail or online. Resumes sent through the mail always need an accompanying letter that briefly introduces you and your resume. The purpose of the cover letter is to get a potential employer to read your resume, just as the purpose of the resume is to get that same potential employer to call you for an interview.

Like your resume, your cover letter should be clean, neat, and direct. A cover letter usually includes the following information:

1. Your name and address (unless it already appears on your personal letterhead) and your phone number(s); see item 7.

2. The date.

3. The name and address of the person and company to whom you are sending your resume.

4. The salutation ("Dear Mr." or "Dear Ms." followed by the person's last name, or "To Whom It May Concern" if you are answering a blind ad).

5. An opening paragraph explaining why you are writing (for example, in response to an ad, as a follow-up to a previous meeting, at the suggestion of someone you both know) and indicating that you are interested in whatever job is being offered.

6. One or more paragraphs that tell why you want to work for the company and what qualifications and experiences you can bring to the position. This is a good place to mention some detail about that particular company that makes you want to work for them; this shows that you have done some research before applying.

7. A final paragraph that closes the letter and invites the reviewer to contact you for an interview. This can be a good place to tell the potential employer which method would be best to use when contacting you. Be sure to give the correct phone number and a good time to reach you, if that is important. You may mention here that your references are available upon request.

8. The closing ("Sincerely" or "Yours truly") followed by your signature in a dark ink, with your name typed under it.

Your cover letter should include all of this information and be no longer than one page in length. The language used should be polite, businesslike, and to the point. Don't attempt to tell your life story in the cover letter; a long and cluttered letter will serve only to annoy the reader. Remember that you need to mention only a few of your accomplishments and skills in the cover letter. The rest of your information is available in your resume. If your cover letter is a success, your resume will be read and all pertinent information reviewed by your prospective employer.

## Producing the Cover Letter

Cover letters should always be individualized because they are always written to specific individuals and companies. Never use a form letter for your cover letter or copy it as you would a resume. Each cover letter should be unique, and as personal and lively as possible. (Of course, once you have written and rewritten your first cover letter until you are satisfied with it, you can certainly use similar wording in subsequent letters. You may want to save a template on your computer for future reference.) Keep a hard copy of each cover letter so you know exactly what you wrote in each one.

After you have written your cover letter, proofread it as thoroughly as you did your resume. Again, spelling or punctuation errors are a sure sign of carelessness, and you don't want that to be a part of your first impression on a prospective employer. This is no time to trust your spellcheck function. Even after going through a spelling and grammar check, your cover letter should be carefully proofread by at least one other person.

Print the cover letter on the same quality bond paper you used for your resume. Remember to sign it, using a good, dark-ink pen. Handle the letter and resume carefully to avoid smudging or wrinkling, and mail them together in an appropriately sized envelope. Many stores sell matching envelopes to coordinate with your choice of bond paper.

Keep an accurate record of all resumes you send out and the results of each mailing. This record can be kept on your computer, in a calendar or notebook, or on file cards. Knowing when a resume is likely to have been received will keep you on track as you make follow-up phone calls.

About a week after mailing resumes and cover letters to potential employers, contact them by telephone. Confirm that your resume arrived and ask whether an interview might be possible. Be sure to record the name of the person you spoke to and any other information you gleaned from the conversation. It is wise to treat the person answering the phone with a great deal of respect; sometimes the assistant or receptionist has the ear of the person doing the hiring.

You should make a great impression with the strong, straightforward resume and personalized cover letter you have just created. Good luck in securing the career of your dreams!

APPENDIX

A

# INTERCULTURAL ASSESSMENT, TRAINING, AND DEVELOPMENT

**D**r. Michael F. Tucker, Ph.D., CMC (Certified Management Consultant) is the president of Tucker International, LLC, which provides a variety of services to multinational corporations and other organizations.

Dr. Tucker is an industrial/organizational psychologist and is the author of the Overseas Assignment Inventory (OAI) and the International Candidate Evaluation (ICE), which are validated instruments used to assess, select, and develop personnel and their spouses and/or families for international assignments.

What follows is extracted from a paper Dr. Tucker wrote entitled "Intercultural Assessment, Training, and Development: A Must for International Assignees and Their Families." (© 2001, Tucker International, Boulder, Colorado). The excerpts are used with his permission.

Abstract: Dealing successfully with intercultural issues is critical for success on an international assignment. This is true not only for employees but for accompanying spouses and children as well. This paper presents a set of well-researched competencies required for successful life in another country, such as open-mindedness, flexibility, and respect for the beliefs of others. [Dr. Tucker presented two case studies in which managers made errors because of a lack of cross-cultural competency. They were unaware of key on-the-job interpersonal dynamics in the two very different countries they were assigned to.] By developing intercultural competency through a professional process of assessment, training, and development for their assignments, international assignees and their families can manage the issues related to these cases more effectively. It is simply not enough to have the requisite technical, managerial, or administrative skills to succeed on an international assignment. Intercultural competency is also required.

Families who are sent on international assignment should be treated as a unit, and the special needs of family members should be incorporated into the professional preparation process. It is well known that an expatriate spouse can make or break an international assignment. If the spouse becomes well-adjusted and happy, the employee can apply full attention to the job. If not, the entire assignment may be disrupted. Involving the spouse and the family in the assessment and training process can go a long way toward ensuring success. [Dr. Tucker's goals are virtually the same as those discussed throughout this book.]

This assessment helps candidates to:

- Honestly assess their current situation to determine if they are ready to take on the challenge of adapting successfully to a different culture.
- Make sure their expectations are realistic about an international assignment, a new job, and especially a new environment and culture.

The most successful expatriates are those who take on an international assignment with motivations that are:

- Positive or forward-looking rather than escaping from something
- Well balanced between job or career and personal development
- Sustaining in ways that can withstand the pressures of life and work overseas

[Dr. Tucker stresses the importance of open and honest communication between spouses when it comes to weighing the pros and cons of an international move, and he also is concerned about children who are facing an overseas relocation.]

The following are the top ten concerns of young people who move to another country:

- Leaving friends
- Making new friends
- Leaving school behind
- What to expect from the new school and fitting in
- Leaving pets behind
- What life will be like
- Not understanding the language
- Being removed from sports activities
- Not liking the new country, climate, customs, and food
- Being afraid

[Something tells me that the children's fears are quite similar to those of their parents! In addition to the assessment process, Dr. Tucker and his associates provide highly personalized training to people who are being groomed for long-term overseas assignments. He's found that careful pre-screening of candidates, combined with predeparture training for those who are selected, greatly increases their chances of succeeding in international assignments.]

APPENDIX

B

# AMERICAN AND CANADIAN UNDERGRADUATE PROGRAMS IN INTERNATIONAL BUSINESS

The following is a sample of American and Canadian colleges and universities that have undergraduate programs in international business, international business marketing, or international finance. Keep in mind that this is not an exhaustive list; an online search or a visit to your local library or career resource center may yield more educational opportunities near you.

Alfred University
Alfred, NY
alfred.edu

American International College
Springfield, MA
aic.edu

American University
Washington, DC
american.edu

Arkansas State University
State University, AR
astate.edu

Auburn University
Auburn, AL
auburn.edu

Baylor University
Waco, TX
baylor.edu

Bernard M. Baruch College of the City University of New York
New York, NY
baruch.cuny.edu

Boston University
Boston, MA
bu.edu

Bowling Green State University
Bowling Green, OH
bgsu.edu

Butler University
Indianapolis, IN
butler.edu

Catholic University of America
Washington, DC
cua.edu

College of New Jersey
Ewing, NJ
tcnj.edu

Concordia University
Montreal, QC
concordia.ca

DePaul University
Chicago, IL
depaul.edu

Dominican College
Orangeburg, NY
dc.edu

Drexel University
Philadelphia, PA
drexel.edu

Florida Atlantic University
Boca Raton, FL
fau.edu

Florida International University
Miami, FL
fiu.edu

Florida State University
Tallahassee, FL
fsu.edu

Fordham University
New York, NY
fordham.edu

Georgetown University
Washington, DC
georgetown.edu

George Washington University
Washington, DC
gwu.edu

Gonzaga University
Spokane, WA
gonzaga.edu

Hofstra University
Hempstead, NY
hofstra.edu

Howard University
Washington, DC
howard.edu

Iona College
New Rochelle, NY
iona.edu

Johnson & Wales University
Providence, RI
jwu.edu

Lehigh University
Bethlehem, PA
lehigh.edu

Long Island University
C.W. Post Campus
Brookville, NY
liu.edu

Louisiana State University
Baton Rouge, LA
lsu.edu

Loyola University New Orleans
New Orleans, LA
loyno.edu

McGill University
Montreal, QC
mcgill.ca

New Mexico State University
Las Cruces, NM
nmsu.edu

New York University
New York, NY
nyu.edu

Northeastern University
Boston, MA
neu.edu

Ohio State University
Columbus, OH
osu.edu

Oklahoma State University
Stillwater, OK
okstate.edu

Oregon State University
Corvallis, OR
orst.edu

Pace University
New York, NY
pace.edu

Pennsylvania State University
Behrend College
Erie, PA
pserie.psu.edu

Pepperdine University
Malibu, CA
pepperdine.edu

Rochester Institute of Technology
Rochester, NY
rit.edu

Roosevelt University
Chicago, IL
roosevelt.edu

Sacred Heart University
Fairfield, CT
sacredheart.edu

Salem College
Winston-Salem, NC
salem.edu

Schiller International University
Dunedin, FL
schiller.edu

Southern New Hampshire University
Manchester, NH
snhu.edu

State University of New York at Plattsburgh
Plattsburgh, NY
plattsburgh.edu

Temple University
Philadelphia, PA
temple.edu

Texas Tech University
Lubbock, TX
ttu.edu

University of Akron
Akron, OH
uakron.edu

University of Arkansas
Fayetteville, AR
uark.edu

University of Baltimore
Baltimore, MD
ubalt.edu

University of Bridgeport
Bridgeport, CT
bridgeport.edu

University of British Columbia
Vancouver, BC
ubc.ca

University of Dayton
Dayton, OH
udayton.edu

University of Georgia
Athens, GA
uga.edu

University of Memphis
Memphis, TN
memphis.edu

University of Montana—Missoula
Missoula, MT
umt.edu

University of Nebraska—Lincoln
Lincoln, NE
unl.edu

University of Nevada—Las Vegas
Las Vegas, NV
unlv.edu

University of Oregon
Eugene, OR
uoregon.edu

University of Ottawa
Ottawa, ON
uottawa.ca

University of Rhode Island
Kingston, RI
uri.edu

University of Texas—Dallas
Richardson, TX
utdallas.edu

Valparaiso University
Valparaiso, IN
valpo.edu

Villanova University
Villanova, PA
vill.edu

Widener University
Chester, PA
widener.edu

# AMERICAN AND CANADIAN GRADUATE PROGRAMS IN INTERNATIONAL BUSINESS

**T**he following is a sample of American and Canadian colleges and universities that have graduate programs in international business. Keep in mind that this is not an exhaustive list; an online search or a visit to your local library or career resource center may yield more educational opportunities near you.

Alliant International University
San Diego, CA
usiu.edu

American InterContinental University
Los Angeles, CA
aiuniv.edu

American University
Washington, DC
american.edu

Argosy University (multiple locations)
argosyu.edu

Azusa Pacific University
Azusa, CA
apu.edu

Babson College
Babson Park, MA
babson.edu

Baldwin-Wallace College
Berea, OH
bw.edu

Baylor University
Waco, TX
baylor.edu

Bentley College
Waltham, MA
bentley.edu

Bernard M. Baruch College of the City University of New York
New York, NY
baruch.cuny.edu

Boston University
Boston, MA
bu.edu

Brandeis University
Waltham, MA
brandeis.edu

California State University—Fullerton
Fullerton, CA
fullerton.edu

California State University—Los Angeles
Los Angeles, CA
calstatela.edu

Central Michigan University
Mount Pleasant, MI
cmich.edu

Claremont Graduate University
Claremont, CA
cgu.edu

Clark University
Worcester, MA
clarku.edu

Columbia University
New York, NY
columbia.edu

DePaul University
Chicago, IL
depaul.edu

Dominican University of California
San Rafael, CA
dominican.edu

Drury University
Springfield, MO
drury.edu

Eastern Michigan University
Ypsilanti, MI
emich.edu

École des Hautes Études Commerciales
Montreal, QC
hec.ca

Fairleigh Dickinson University
Florham-Madison Campus
Madison, NJ
fdu.edu

Florida International University
Miami, FL
fiu.edu

George Washington University
Washington, DC
gwu.edu

Georgia State University
Atlanta, GA
gsu.edu

Hawaii Pacific University
Honolulu, HI
hpu.edu

Hofstra University
Hempstead, NY
hofstra.edu

Illinois Institute of Technology
Chicago, IL
iit.edu

Indiana University—Bloomington
Bloomington, IN
iub.edu

John Marshall Law School
Chicago, IL
jmls.edu

Johns Hopkins University
Washington, DC
jhu.edu

Johnson & Wales University
Providence, RI
jwu.edu

Mercy College
Dobbs Ferry, NY
mercynet.edu

Monterey Institute of International Studies
Monterey, CA
miis.edu

National Technological University
Fort Collins, CO
petersons.com/ntu

New School University
New York, NY
newschool.edu

New York University
New York, NY
nyu.edu

Pace University
New York, NY
pace.edu

Pepperdine University
Malibu, CA
pepperdine.edu

Point Park College
Pittsburgh, PA
ppc.edu

Portland State University
Portland, OR
pdx.edu

Quinnipiac University
Hamden, CT
quinnipiac.edu

Rochester Institute of Technology
Rochester, NY
rit.edu

Roosevelt University
Chicago, IL
roosevelt.edu

Rutgers, The State University of New Jersey
Newark, NJ
rutgers.edu

St. Edward's University
Austin, TX
stedwards.edu

St. John's University
Jamaica, NY
stjohns.edu

Saint Joseph's University
Philadelphia, PA
sju.edu

Saint Louis University
St. Louis, MO
slu.edu

San Diego State University
San Diego, CA
sdsu.edu

School for International Training
Brattleboro, VT
sit.edu

Seattle University
Seattle, WA
seattleu.edu

Southern New Hampshire University
Manchester, NH
snhu.edu

Temple University
Philadelphia, PA
temple.edu

Texas A&M International University
Laredo, TX
tamiu.edu

Thunderbird
The American Graduate School of International Management
Glendale, AZ
t-bird.edu

Tufts University
Medford, MA
tufts.edu

Université de Sherbrooke
Sherbrooke, QC
usherb.ca

Université du Québec
École nationale d'administration publique
Quebec, QC
enap.uquebec.ca

University of Colorado—Denver
Denver, CO
cudenver.edu

University of Connecticut
Storrs, CT
uconn.edu

University of Dallas
Irving, TX
udallas.edu

University of Florida
Gainesville, FL
ufl.edu

University of Hawaii—Manoa
Honolulu, HI
hawaii.edu

University of Kentucky
Lexington, KY
uky.edu

University of Maryland University College
College Park, MD
umuc.edu

University of Memphis
Memphis, TN
memphis.edu

University of Ottawa
Ottawa, ON
uottawa.ca

University of Pennsylvania
Philadelphia, PA
upenn.edu

University of Phoenix
Phoenix, AZ
phoenix.edu

University of Pittsburgh
Pittsburgh, PA
pitt.edu

University of St. Thomas
St. Paul, MN
stthomas.edu

University of South Carolina
Columbia, SC
sc.edu

University of Southern California
Los Angeles, CA
usc.edu

University of Toledo
Toledo, OH
utoledo.edu

University of Tulsa
Tulsa, OK
utulsa.edu

University of Washington
Seattle, WA
washington.edu

University of Wisconsin—Madison
Madison, WI
wisc.edu

# ADDITIONAL RESOURCES*

ABI/Inform on Disc
SilverPlatter
Ovid Technologies
New York, NY

*Advertising Career Directory*
Visible Ink Press
Gale Research, Inc.
Detroit, MI (out of print: 5th ed. 1992)

*America's Corporate Families*
Dun & Bradstreet Information Services
Bethlehem, PA (last edition 1993)

*Guide to America's Federal Jobs* (2nd ed.)
JIST Publishing
Indianapolis, IN

*The Best Companies for Minorities*
Lawrence Graham
Plume Books
New York, NY

*Compiled by Monica Stoll, Editor, VGM Career Books

*Burrelle's Media Directory*
Burrelle's Media Directories
Livingston, NJ

*Business and Finance Career Directory*
Visible Ink Press/Gale Group
Detroit, MI

*Business Rankings Annual*
Gale Group
Detroit, MI

*The Career Guide: Dun's Employment Opportunities Directory*
Dun & Bradstreet Information Services
Bethlehem, PA

*Career Information Center* (8th edition)
Macmillan Library Reference
Gale Group
Macmillan Library Reference
Detroit, MI

*Careers Encyclopedia*
VGM Career Books
Chicago, IL

*Careers in Business*
*Careers in Communications*
*Careers in Finance*
*Careers in Government*
VGM Career Books
Chicago, IL

*Careers in the Nonprofit Sector: Doing Well by Doing Good*
Terry McAdam
The Taft Group
Washington, DC

*The Chronicle of Higher Education*
Washington, DC

*College to Career: The Guide to Job Opportunities*
Joyce Mitchell
The College Board
New York, NY
collegeboard.com

*The Corporate Address Book*
Michael Levine
G.P. Putnam's Sons
New York, NY

*Directory of American Firms Operating in Foreign Countries*
(16th ed. 2001)
World Trade Academy Press
New York, NY

*Directory of Corporate Affiliations*
LexisNexis
Div. of Reed-Elsevier
Albany, NY

*Effective Answers to Interview Questions* (video)
JIST Publishing
Indianapolis, IN

*Encyclopedia of Associations*
Encyclopedia of Business Information Sources
Gale Group
Detroit, MI

*Federal Career Opportunities*
Gordon Press Publishers
New York, NY

*Federal Jobs Digest*
Breakthrough Publications
Osinning, NY
jobsfed.com

*Federal Times*
6883 Commercial Drive
Springfield, VA 22159
federaltimes.com

*Fedworld*
U.S. Department of Commerce
Springfield, VA
fedworld.com

*Flying High in Travel*
John Wiley & Sons
New York, NY

*Foreign Consular Offices in the United States*
U.S. Department of State
Washington, DC

*Handbook for Business and Management Careers*
VGM Career Books
Chicago, IL

*The Complete Guide to International Jobs and Careers*
Ron and Caryl Krannich
Impact Publications
Manassas Park, VA

*NewsLinks*
International Schools Services
Princeton, NJ

*Occupational Outlook Handbook*
*Occupational Outlook Quarterly*
U.S. Department of Labor
Bureau of Labor Statistics
Washington, DC

*101 Challenging Government Jobs for College Graduates*
Hungry Minds/Wiley
New York, NY

*Opportunities in Federal Government Careers*
*Opportunities in Marketing Careers*
*Opportunities in Nonprofit Organizations*
*Opportunities in Sales Careers*
*Opportunities in Technical Sales Careers*
*Opportunities in Telecommunications Careers*
VGM Career Books
Chicago, IL

*U.S. Industry & Trade Outlook*
U.S. Government Printing Office
Washington, D.C.

*World Chamber of Commerce Directory*
Loveland, CO

International Business Resource Desk
globaledge.msu.edu/ibrd/ibrd.asp

United States Council for International Business
uscib.org

International Business Resource Connection
ibrc.bschool.ukans.edu

International Business Forum
ibf.com

The Internationalist: The Center for International Business and Travel.
internationalist.com/welcome.php3

International Business Opportunities Centre (Canadian)
iboc.gc.ca

Internet Public Library: International Business
ipl.org/div/subject/browse/bus45.00.00

# RECOMMENDED
# READINGS

The majority of the books listed here are readily available in libraries or at booksellers, including online outfits (such as Amazon.com). Some may be out of print or have multiple publishers, so in those cases I haven't listed the publisher. In any event, none of my students has had difficulty obtaining a copy of these titles.

## NONFICTION

- *International Job Finder: Where the Jobs Are Worldwide* by Daniel Lauber. This may be the most ambitious undertaking in the area of career publishing. The book, which is put out by Planning Communications, has over 1,200 potential contacts. The author strives valiantly to provide current web addresses, and gives you plenty of information, including up-to-date danger spots around the globe.
- *Working Abroad* by the editors of *Transitions Abroad* magazine. I've mentioned this gem elsewhere in this book. If it isn't in your library, call 1-800-293-0373.
- *Global Studies* series. These marvelous books are published by McGraw-Hill/Dushkin. Nation by nation, they discuss the various geographic regions of the world. Every volume begins with a quick

look at the United States and Canada, which provides the reader with useful standards of comparison (population, land mass, literacy rates, per capita income, and so on) in order to assess the extent to which the country(s) is similar to us.

Each volume contains a fast-moving historical narrative and concludes with reprints of recent, relevant articles concerning economics, politics, and social issues. These books will give you an excellent overview of what life is like in other countries. Note: they are frequently revised, so check to make sure you have the most current edition(s).

- *The Forgotten Founders: Rethinking the History of the Old West* by Stewart L. Udall (published by Island Press). I was once chatting (in French, our only common language) with a Bedouin shepherd in the Sinai desert. He asked me where I was from, and I said Denver. "Ah," he replied, "Dynasty!" It turned out that he'd seen reruns of the old series, ostensibly set in Denver, when he made periodic visits to an oasis with a TV. Regrettably, many people around the world have a distorted vision of the United States, thanks to television shows. (Don't get me started on "The Dukes of Hazzard!") Unfortunately, so do many U.S. citizens. This short but highly informative volume should fill in quite a few blanks and give the lie to the Manifest Destiny theory.
- *Little Brown Brother* by Leon Wolff. Speaking of Manifest Destiny, this history of the United States' takeover of the Philippines, a country I had the privilege of living and working in for two years, has wonderfully timely insights, even though the events described took place more than a century ago.
- *Resistance, Rebellion, and Death* by Albert Camus. Not everyone in a foreign land is likely to share your views. This is a useful primer for testing ideas: yours and the author's.

## FICTION

At first blush, a section on fiction would seem to have no place in a business book. However, as my students will tell you, novels serve a useful purpose: letting you hear the "voices" of people, rather than confining yourself solely to numbers. In the process, you'll learn about history, customs, and traditions. This knowledge will serve you in good stead when you are working with and living among people from the countries in which the stories are set. I'm confining myself to Asia and Europe, the two places where you're most likely to find work.

## Asia

China has changed in terms of opening up to Western trade, including bringing in consultants from, among other places, the United States and Canada. Even so, an appreciation of China's history and culture is useful, as it will help you to grasp how things work, including the Eastern concept of time.

- Robert Van Gulik's *Judge Dee* mystery stories are novels written by a Dutch diplomat who spent many years in Asia. They're loosely based on the life of a seventh century magistrate and court official. The books are excellent primers in the areas of history, philosophy, politics, and religion. Either *The Chinese Nail Murders* or *Poets and Murder* are good ones to start with. Caution: they're addictive!
- *White Lotus* by John Hersey. The premise is that the United States was defeated by China in an early twentieth century war, which, given what happened in Vietnam, isn't all that far-fetched. The book deals mainly with Caucasian slaves from the United States who have been shipped to China. They're striving for equality, determined to prove that they're just as good as their Chinese masters.
- *The Call*, also by John Hersey. This traces Chinese history throughout most of the twentieth century, as seen through the eyes of a Christian missionary from the United States. This novel, like *White Lotus*, promotes serious thinking.

    Then there are two relatively recent gems:
- *Himalayan Dhaba* by Craig Joseph Danner (published by Dutton). India has, arguably, the world's largest middle class. It also has a great deal of incredible poverty, and this novel straddles both worlds.
- *Red Dream* by Victoria Brooks (published by Greatest Escapes Publishing). This is Vietnam's *Gone with the Wind*. It fills in a few historical blanks.

### Europe

- *All Quiet on the Western Front* by Erich Maria Remarque. This may well be the very best book about war. Like all of the European books I'll recommend in this section, it focuses largely on the losing side. Thus, it provides you with a totally different perspective from standard history books.

  One of my global marketing students opted to write a report on this book. When she came into class one day, it was plain to see that she'd been crying. I thought there had been a tragedy in her family. She said, "I don't want to finish this book—the war's almost over, and I know he's going to die, and I don't want to see it!" She began crying anew. I excused her from reading the last few pages, because she'd gotten the main point of the exercise—in war, as well as in business, the "numbers" represent people.

- *Billiards at Half-Past Nine* by Heinrich Boll. The bulk of twentieth-century German history is covered, as witnessed by a fascinating family.

- *A Sailor of Austria* by John Biggins. The hero's country is not only defeated in WWI, it loses its national identity. The book provides a helpful and, on the whole, rather enjoyable history lesson.

- *The Age of Reason* by Jean-Paul Sartre. This is the first volume of his WWII trilogy, and it's set in France during the last few years before the German invasion. Sartre was a major philosopher, and reading this book is an intriguing way of learning about existentialism, which is, putting it mildly, about as European as it gets.

## CONCLUSION

If you've steeped yourself in the books I've suggested, you'll have been exposed to some very different ways of looking at things. In the process of tracking the books down, you may well have some interesting discussions with librarians and booksellers, leading you to other books and more new ideas. The key is to keep learning and growing.

# ABOUT THE AUTHOR

Edward J. Halloran holds degrees from Norwalk Community College in Connecticut, Columbia College, and Webster University. He is also a graduate of the American Academy of Dramatic Arts in New York City.

He has extensive corporate and consulting experience in the international sector and has lived and worked overseas.

Mr. Halloran has taught business, drama, and interpersonal relations courses at a number of schools. Since 1985, he has been an adjunct professor at Columbia College's Extended Studies center in Aurora, Colorado. He teaches courses in marketing, management, and international business.

He also works as a Denver-based freelance correspondent for a number of print and broadcast entities, chiefly Bloomberg Radio & Television and Agence France Presse. Halloran's additional credits include: Fox Online, Metro Networks, CourtTV.com, PublicInteractive.com, Monitor Radio, Scripps Howard, and the Armed Forces Network.

He is the author of several nonfiction books and serves as the international editor for *Marketing Journal*.